9/92

D0046442

TELECOMMUNICATIONS

Telecommunications
FROM TELEGRAPHS TO MODEMS

by Christopher Lampton

FRANKLIN WATTS/1991
NEW YORK/LONDON/TORONTO/SYDNEY
A VENTURE BOOK

Photographs courtesy of: Historical Pictures Service: pp. 13, 53; Peter Arnold, Inc.: pp. 21, 73 (Leonard Lessin); Bettmann Archive: p. 41; Jeff Greenberg: p. 46; Bell Laboratories: p. 59; AT&T Archives: p. 66; Photo Researchers, Inc.: p. 98 (Spencer Grant), 101 (Blair Seitz); 3M Photo: p. 114; GE Information Services: p. 125.

Library of Congress Cataloging-in-Publication Data

Lampton, Christopher.
Telecommunications : from telegraphs to modems / by Christopher Lampton.
p.   cm.—(A Venture book)
Includes bibliographical references and index.
Summary: Discusses the many forms of electronic communication with an emphasis on the development of transmission using analog and digital signals.
ISBN 0-531-12527-0
1. Telecommunication—Juvenile literature.
[1. Telecommunication.]   I. Title.
TK102.4.L36   1991
621.382—dc20   90-48230 CIP AC

CONTENTS

TELECOMMUNICATIONS

PROLOGUE: COMMUNICATIONS AND INFORMATION

Over and over we are told that we live in an Information Age, as though this were something new. In fact, living organisms—human and otherwise—have always lived in a world filled with information. And that information is as important to us as the air we breathe and the food we eat. Without information, we would die.

But what is information? Is it the headlines on the morning newspaper? Or the blaring voice of a radio disk jockey? Or the columns of numbers and words on the video display of a computer?

In fact, information is all those things and more. To put it as simply as possible, information is anything that tells you something you didn't already know. If you didn't know what information was, for instance, then that last sentence was information. On the other hand, if you have already read that definition in half a dozen other books, then that sentence wasn't very informative—that is, it wasn't information. Not to you, at least.

Information can come from lots of sources. The morning weather forecast may tell you that it's going to rain when you expected it to be sunny. (Better get on the phone and cancel that big picnic!) You may open your eyes one morning to find that you're in a strange room rather than the familiar bedroom you normally wake up in. (Maybe you fell asleep on the living room sofa while watching a late movie.) A sudden cold sensation on your back may tell you that the shirt you just put on is still wet from the laundry. (Put on another one before you catch cold!)

In each case, you have learned something you didn't know before—that is, you have received information. Of course, not all information will be of equal importance to you. The forecast for rain will be of less importance if you plan to stay inside all day than if you are headed for the beach. And the wet shirt will be irrelevant if you plan to jump fully dressed into a swimming pool. (Okay, so that's not very likely—but it's been known to happen!)

HOW WE OBTAIN INFORMATION

We receive information from the world around us through our senses. Each sense receives information in a different form. Our sense of sight, for instance, receives information in the form of visible light. Our sense of hearing receives information in the form of sound waves. A person who lacked all senses could receive no information whatsoever from the outside world and could only survive if taken care of on a nearly continual basis. Fortunately, almost everybody has the use of some of their senses—and people who lack one or two senses can use other senses to compensate.

All living organisms—even plants and one-celled animals—have sensory organs of some kind or other, no matter how rudimentary. These sensory organs are necessary because the world around these organisms is in a constant state of change and they need information about that change if they are to survive in that world. A plant growing in dry soil, for instance, must know about that dryness so it can send its roots deeper in search of moisture.

As far as we know, the first living organisms on this planet four billion years ago were no more than complicated molecules—chains of atoms—floating in shallow pools of water. They survived by "eating" (that is, breaking apart) other, simpler molecules for "food." At first, these shallow pools of water were rich with these simpler molecules and the early living organisms had only to wait while the food came to them. But as the food supply dwindled and competition with other organisms increased, it became necessary to seek out food—which required some sort of information, however crude, about where the food was at any given time. And as these organisms learned to eat *each other* for food, it became necessary to have information about other organisms, so that they could be either located and eaten or carefully avoided.

Billions of years later, the distant descendants of these primitive organisms are still doing much the same thing—predators seeking prey, prey avoiding predators, and everybody looking for food—but their methods of acquiring information are vastly more sophisticated. A sharp-eyed eagle uses its sense of sight to spot a tiny (and edible) mouse hundreds of feet below. An antelope leaps away at the sound of stealthy movement across the veldt. A dog comes running when it smells its dinner being spooned into a tray.

But modern living organisms can do something that the first living organisms could not. They can *create* information, originating messages and sending them to other living organisms. Prairie dogs cry out to warn other prairie dogs that a predator is near. Romantically inclined female dogs produce molecules called pheromones to attract potential mates. Bees engage in elaborate dances to tell other bees where pollen rich flowers can be found.

No other living creature, though, is as good at sending (and receiving) messages as human beings are. We chatter incessantly, chafing impatiently when we must spend a half hour in silence. We write letters, make phone calls, gesture with our hands and faces—all as a way of sending messages to other human beings. Because humans are social animals, our survival depends on the cooperation of other human beings—and cooperation requires the constant transmission of information from one individual to another. ("Pass the butter, sis." "Sell when the Dow Jones hits 2,000, Bob." "Fire when ready, Gridley.")

MODES OF COMMUNICATION

The act of sending messages between individuals is called *communication*. The most common form of communication among human beings is *speech,* the sending of messages by voice. No one knows when and where speech originated, but it was probably between 50,000 and 500,000 years ago, when anatomically modern human beings came into existence. (Other animals, such as chimpan-

An early technique of signaling
the alphabet with torches (ca. 150 B.C.).
Humans have always sought
improved means of communicating
at a distance.

zees, have a rudimentary form of speech, but it is so much less sophisticated than the kind practiced by human beings that it might as well be classed as a different form of communication.)

Speech isn't the only kind of communication practiced by human beings. Writing, for instance, is a kind of written speech, but it can do things that speech cannot. A written message can survive for many years before it is read, while a spoken message is lost (except in the memory of those who hear it) the instant after it is completed.

Painting is also a form of communication, as are sign language, semaphores and even smoke signals. No other animal communicates in as many ways as human beings—or sends messages as complex and sophisticated.

Thousands of years ago, when people lived in tribes of a few dozen individuals, communication was easy. If you wanted to talk to someone, you went to that person and talked. If the person you wanted to talk to lived in a neighboring tribe, you went to that tribe and sought him out—or gave the message to someone who was going to that tribe.

But as time passed and human beings spread out across the face of the earth, it became necessary to communicate over longer and longer distances. Written language probably was invented in part as a way of sending messages, in the form of letters and other documents, over distances of hundreds and thousands of miles. For many centuries, written messages were the primary means of communicating over long distances. Unfortunately, this was a slow way of sending messages. When greater speed was needed—during wartime, for instance—faster methods had to be used, such

14

as semaphore relays. But these were awkward and expensive forms of communication, at best.

TELECOMMUNICATION: "COMMUNICATION AT A DISTANCE"

Then, in the first half of the nineteenth century, a new method of communicating over long distances was developed—and a communications revolution began. We call that new method *telecommunications*.

The word *telecommunications* literally means "communication at a distance." In that sense, written messages are a form of telecommunication. But we usually reserve the term to describe *electronic communications*—that is, messages that are carried either by an *electric current* or by *electromagnetic radiation*. This form of telecommunications has existed for barely more than a century and a half, but it has had a profound effect on the world that we live in.

In this book, we'll talk about the many forms of electronic communication, the things that those forms have in common, and the ways in which they have changed the world. We'll also talk about new forms of telecommunication that are even now on the horizon—and how they may change the world of the next century as profoundly as existing means of telecommunication have changed the world in this century. Perhaps most importantly, we'll talk about a communications revolution that is taking place right at this very moment: the shift from so-called *analog* communications to *digital* communications and why this important shift may change the way we interact with the world around us!

PART ONE
ANALOG
TELECOMMUNICATIONS

1
WAVES, ELECTRICITY, AND INFORMATION

In 1833, the volcano Krakatoa erupted on a small island in the Indian Ocean, between Java and Sumatra. The sound created by the explosion was so intense that it swept nearly halfway around the world. In California, a noise like a burst of gunfire was reported.

In a few hours, the sound of the Krakatoa explosion had traversed oceans, to be heard on distant continents. The sound arrived long before news of the event.

Talk about telecommunications!

When you talk, the sound of your voice radiates outward at a speed of more than 1,000 feet per second, just like the sound of the Krakatoa explosion—but it doesn't travel nearly as far. If it did, you wouldn't need a telephone to talk to friends and relatives in faraway places.

Sound is a kind of wave. Waves like to travel, and they usually travel fairly fast. In fact, as we'll see later, the fastest thing in the universe is a kind of wave. (Actually, if you ask a physicist, he'll tell you that everything in the universe—including you, this book, and the chair you're sitting on—is a kind of wave. But that's a detail we'll ignore in this book.) And, as sound waves prove, waves are a reliable means of transmitting information.

But if we plan to transmit information over long distances, we'll need something that travels farther than a sound wave. The explosion of Krakatoa was a freak; most sound waves never get farther than the room in which they are created.

WHAT IS A WAVE?

Okay, you probably know what a wave is already. It's what happens when you sit down too quickly in the bathtub. Or it's what you put a surfboard on top of at the beach.

But have you ever thought about how waves behave? Or how you would describe a wave to someone who had never seen one? Or how you could use a wave to carry information? If not, pay close attention to the rest of this chapter. We're going to look at some concepts that are crucial to the discussion of telecommunications in the rest of this book.

Imagine a perfectly still pool of water. You take a small stone and throw it into the center of the pool. You hear a soft splashing noise as the stone enters the water. Perfectly circular ripples move outward from the point of impact.

Congratulations! You've made waves!

That was pretty easy, you think—and, indeed, it was. All you did was supply the energy that got the wave started. From that point on, the natural processes of gravitation and wave motion took over and kept the waves going.

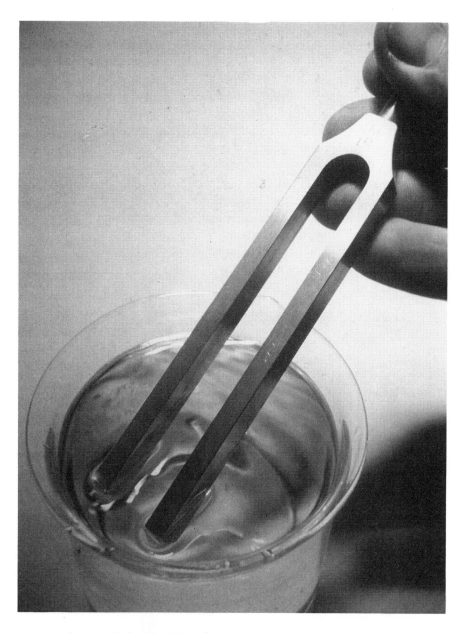

A tuning fork placed in a glass of
water: a "visible" sound wave

You supplied the energy by lifting the stone off of the ground, against the force of gravity. When you let go of the stone, gravity pulled it back toward the ground (with an assist from your pitching arm) and drew the stone into the water. Most of the energy in the falling stone then went toward pushing the water down to make room for the stone.

Water doesn't like to be compressed, the way that a sponge does (to choose but one example). When the stone pushes on the water, the water moves out of the way to make room for the stone, which creates a little "hill" of water surrounding the stone. But gravity almost immediately pulls this little hill back down, the way it pulled the stone down. This displaces still more water and another little hill of water forms directly outside the first hill. The process repeats itself over and over, as the hill moves farther and farther away from the point at which the stone fell.

Meanwhile, the water at the point where the stone fell rises up and down, producing still more of these moving hills of water, until it runs out of energy. Each of these moving hills is, of course, a wave.

Although the wave itself moves sideways fairly rapidly, the water that makes up the wave doesn't move very far at all. Mostly, it moves up and down. It's the wave itself—the pattern of up and down motion in the water—that actually travels. Because the wave pattern moves outward in all directions simultaneously from its source (in this case, the point at which the stone entered the water), we say that the waves are *radiating*. We could even describe the waves as a form of *radiation*, though this term is usually reserved for other types of waves and wavelike phenomena. (This doesn't mean that water waves or sound waves are a form of nuclear radiation, like that associated with nu-

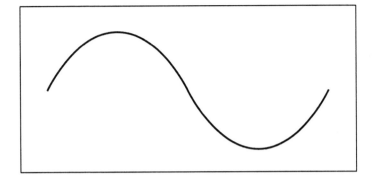

Figure 1. Sine wave

clear bombs and atomic reactors. They won't cause radiation poisoning or radiation-induced cancer.)

Aside from the pattern of wave motion, something else moves along with the wave: energy. The energy that you put into the stone by picking it up and hurling it into the water is transferred from the stone to the wave as the stone plummets into the water. The wave then carries that energy out toward the farthest edges of the pool. It is this energy that makes the wave move. As the circle-shaped waves grow larger and larger, however, this energy becomes spread out over a wider and wider area—and the wave becomes weaker, until it is little more than the faintest ripple on the surface of the water. Finally, it disappears altogether.

The curved line in Figure 1 is a simple representation of a wave. Specifically, it is the kind of wave called a *sine wave*, in honor of the mathematical equation used to describe it. Although waves in the real world are rarely as perfect and smooth as the one shown here, the water wave we described above would probably look pretty much like a sine wave—if we could freeze it in time and slice open a cross section of the pool of water so that we could examine the wave from one side.

23

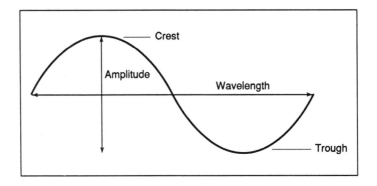

Figure 2. Wave terminology

There are certain terms that we use to describe waves, as illustrated in Figure 2. The high point of the wave, for instance, is the *crest,* while the low point is the *trough.* The distance from one crest to the next (or one trough to the next) is called the *wavelength.* The height of the wave is called the *amplitude.*

The number of wave crests (or troughs) that pass a given point in one second is called the *frequency* of the wave. Frequency and wavelength are closely related. Assuming that two different waves are moving at the same speed, they can only have different frequencies if they have different wavelengths. If one of the waves has a shorter wavelength than the other, then more wave crests will pass a given point in one second—and the frequency will be higher. If one has a longer wavelength than the other, then fewer wave crests will pass a given point in one second—and the frequency will be lower. All other things being equal, as the wavelength goes up, the frequency of the wave goes down—and vice versa.

The frequency of a wave is measured in *cycles per second,* where *cycle* refers to the entire motion of the wave from one crest to the next. More commonly, however, the term *Hertz* (or *Hz*, for short) is used instead of "cycles per second," in honor of the German inventor Heinrich Hertz. (We'll have more to say about Hertz in Chapter Three.) If 10 wave crests (or troughs) are passing a given point every second, we say that the wave has a frequency of 10 Hz. When frequencies become very large, we add metric prefixes to the number of Hertz. For instance, *kilohertz (KHz)* means "thousands of cycles per second," *megahertz (MHz)* means "millions of cycles per second," and *gigahertz (Ghz)* means "billions of cycles per second." Water waves don't ordinarily have frequencies this high, but other types of waves do.

There is one more characteristic that can be used to distinguish one wave from another: the *phase*. This is a slightly more difficult concept than wavelength, amplitude and frequency, because it has to do not with the shape of the wave but with its position in space relative to other waves. Sine waves, like circles, can be measured in degrees, as shown in Figure 3. Thus, the two waves in Figure 4 can be described as being 180 degrees *out of phase* with one another.

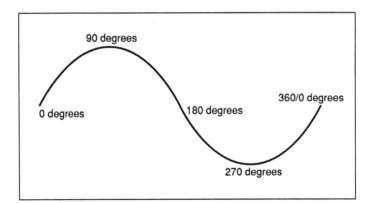

Figure 3. Wave phases

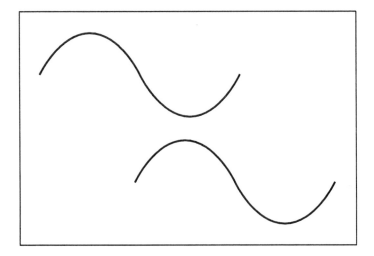

Figure 4. Two waves that are
180 degrees out of phase

To understand the importance of phase, imagine that you throw two stones simultaneously into the still pool of water, roughly three feet apart. Waves radiate outward in perfect circles from both points. Where waves radiating from one point meet waves radiating from the other point, something interesting happens. They begin to create geometric patterns that look nothing like the original waves. When this happens, we say that the waves are *interfering* with one another.

Looked at more closely, the waves are *reinforcing* and *canceling* one another. When two waves come together, they join forces to create a brand new wave that combines the characteristics of both waves. The amplitude of the new wave at each point is the sum of the amplitudes of the two original waves at that point. When two crests come together, they combine to form a supercrest, higher than either original crest. In the same way, when

26

two troughs come together, they combine to form a supertrough, deeper than either original trough. And when a crest and a trough of the same amplitude come together, they simply cancel one another out, leaving nothing but flat water.

When two sine waves come together to form a combined wave, the resulting wave is generally far more complex than any simple sine wave—and thus we call the result a *complex wave.*

In the real world, almost all waves are complex waves. All complex waves are made up of two or more combined sine waves. Using a mathematical technique known as the *Fourier transform* (in honor of Jean-Baptiste Fourier, the nineteenth-century French mathematician who invented the technique), it is actually possible to break any complex wave apart into the sine waves that make it up.

INFORMATION WAVES

Think you know enough about waves now? Want to move on to something else? Well, be patient, because there's one more thing we need to know about waves: how they can be used to carry information.

Information, as we saw in the introduction, is anything that tells you something you didn't already know. Although it may not be obvious, this means that information is about change. If things never changed, there would be no information. If the weather was the same every day, weather forecasts would cease to inform. ("The weather for the tri-state area will be sunny and clear today—for the 5,678th day in a row.") The sentence "AAAAAAAAAAAAAAAAAAAAAAAA" tells you nothing except that somebody must like the letter *A* a lot—and it tells you that in the first one or two characters. A low-pitched droning noise that goes on for many hours carries much less information than a single spoken sentence. And so on.

It follows that, in order to convey information, something must be able to change. When you speak, for instance, the pitch of your voice must constantly change—and it is that change that carries information. Unlike our sentence full of A's in the last paragraph, an informative sentence contains a variety of letters and words—and those letters and words change from one sentence in a paragraph to the next. If every sentence, paragraph and book in the world contained exactly the same words in exactly the same order, there would be no point in reading more than one sentence, paragraph or book. They would all contain exactly the same information—and therefore they would cease containing information at all once you'd read one. Reading more wouldn't tell you anything you didn't already know.

Thus, information and change go hand in hand. To make a wave carry information, we must constantly change the wave, the way the author of a book such as this one constantly changes the words in each successive sentence instead of repeating the same words over and over again. A perfect, unchanging sine wave tells us nothing except its frequency (or wavelength), amplitude and phase—and we know all three of those things almost immediately. A sine wave becomes uninformative very quickly.

There are only three things that we can change about a wave—the frequency (or wavelength, which changes with the frequency), the amplitude and the phase. But by changing one or more of these things in the proper way, we can use a wave to transmit any message that we like, no matter how lengthy or complicated. Changing a wave so that it can carry a message is called *modulation*—that is, we *modulate* the wave. Of course, we can't just modulate the wave at random, because random changes have no meaning. We must change the wave according to a prearranged pattern—a secret code, if you will.

THE DWELLERS IN THE LAKE

To understand how wave modulation works, imagine a race of underwater beings who live at the bottom of a lake. We'll call them the Lakedwellers. On the shores of the lake live a race of air-breathing beings, whom we'll call the Shoredwellers. The Lakedwellers and Shoredwellers live in friendly cooperation, with the Lakedwellers supplying the Shoredwellers with seafood and the Shoredwellers supplying the Lakedwellers with carbonated beverages.

Unfortunately, they have trouble communicating with one another. Shoredwellers can spend only seconds under the water before they need to come up for air and the Lakedwellers will die like beached fish if they leave the water. They could send written messages to each other, of course, but ink tends to get soggy underwater. So the Lakedwellers invent a method of communication involving water waves.

To create waves, they build a giant underwater wheel with a crank attached. Every time they turn the wheel, it moves a piston up and down. For one complete 360-degree turn of the wheel, the piston completes one up-and-down movement. A set of adjustable gears between the wheel and the piston determines how far up and down the piston moves.

29

Because the piston displaces water every time it rises, it creates waves. And the Lakedwellers have complete control over the waves that they are producing:

• They can control the frequency and wavelength of the waves by turning the wheel at different speeds. Turn it faster and the frequency increases (reducing the wavelength). Turn it slower and the frequency decreases (increasing the wavelength).

• By adjusting the gears they can change the amplitude of the waves. The greater the up-and-down motion of the piston, the greater the amplitude of the waves that they are creating. The smaller the up-and-down motion of the piston, the smaller the amplitude of the waves that they are creating.

• By suddenly reversing the direction of the wheel in mid-turn, they can change the phase of the wave. For instance, suddenly reversing the wheel when the piston is halfway to its full height will create a wave that is 180 degrees out of phase with the previous wave. (Note that 180 degrees is one half of 360 degrees.) Reversing the wheel when the piston is one-fourth of the way to its full height will create a wave that is 90 degrees out of phase with the previous wave. (90 degrees is one-fourth of 360 degrees.) A similar effect could be produced by simply not turning the wheel for a fraction of the time it normally takes to turn it. For instance, pausing for one-fourth of the time it takes to produce a single carrier wave and then turning the wheel again in the same direction would produce a wave 90 degrees out of phase with the carrier wave.

In each case, the Lakedwellers are modulating the wave. Because the first kind of modulation involves changing the frequency of the wave, we call it *frequency modulation,* or *FM* for short. Because the second kind of modulation involves changing the amplitude of the wave, we call it *amplitude modulation,* or *AM* for short. And because the third kind of modulation involves changing the phase of the wave, we call it *phase modulation.* (If the terms AM and FM sound suspiciously familiar, they should. As we'll see in Chapter Three, AM and FM radio broadcasts use amplitude modulation and frequency modulation, respectively, to encode sound information on radio waves.)

The waves created by the water wheel radiate outward from the center of the lake, where the Lakedwellers live, and eventually reach the shores of the lake, where the Shoredwellers live. The Shoredwellers use sensitive instruments to measure the frequency, amplitude, and phase of the waves. In this way, they can detect any changes in the waves created by the Lakedwellers.

When the Lakedwellers want to send a message to the Shoredwellers, they first begin rotating the wheel in a steady, even motion. This produces a more or less constant sine wave that can be detected by the Shoredwellers. Because the Lakedwellers are going to use this wave to carry information, we call it the *carrier wave.*

Then, when the Lakedwellers are ready, they send their message by making changes in this carrier wave. We said a moment ago that information involved change. And, indeed, the message sent by the Lakedwellers is encoded not so much in the wave itself as in the changes in the wave. How can such changes be used to encode a message? There are almost an infinite number of ways. We'll look at a few simple-to-understand (if not necessarily practical) methods in this chapter. Then, in later chapters, we'll look at methods that are really used in the world of telecommunications.

ENCODING INFORMATION

At some point, you've probably seen examples of coded messages—in cryptograms, for instance. In such a message, one letter of the alphabet is used to stand for another letter. As written, the messages looks like nonsense, but if you know what the code is, you can substitute the real letters for their stand-ins and read the message. For instance, try using the simple substitution code in Figure 5 to decode the following secret message:

DZEVH XZM YV NLWFOZGVW

To translate the message, look up each letter on the left side of one of the two columns in Figure 5, then substitute the corresponding letter from the right-hand column.

A	–	Z	N	–	M
B	–	Y	O	–	L
C	–	X	P	–	K
D	–	W	Q	–	J
E	–	V	R	–	I
F	–	U	S	–	H
G	–	T	T	–	G
H	–	S	U	–	F
I	–	R	V	–	E
J	–	Q	W	–	D
K	–	P	X	–	C
L	–	O	Y	–	B
M	–	N	Z	–	A

Figure 5: A Simple Substitution Code

A	–	1	N	–	14	a	–	–1	n	–	–14
B	–	2	O	–	15	b	–	–2	o	–	–15
C	–	3	P	–	16	c	–	–3	p	–	–16
D	–	4	Q	–	17	d	–	–4	q	–	–17
E	–	5	R	–	18	e	–	–5	r	–	–18
F	–	6	S	–	19	f	–	–6	s	–	–19
G	–	7	T	–	20	g	–	–7	t	–	–20
H	–	8	U	–	21	h	–	–8	u	–	–21
I	–	9	V	–	22	i	–	–9	v	–	–22
J	–	10	W	–	23	j	–	–10	w	–	–23
K	–	11	X	–	24	k	–	–11	x	–	–24
L	–	12	Y	–	25	l	–	–12	y	–	–25
M	–	13	Z	–	26	m	–	–13	z	–	–26

0 – BLANK SPACE

Figure 6: A Simple Amplitude Modulation Code

A substitution code such as this need not rely on substituting letters of the alphabet for other letters. Instead, we could substitute pictures or numbers (a technique we'll study in more detail when we discuss digital telecommunications) or even, well, various characteristics of a wave.

Suppose, for instance, that the Lakedwellers decide to use amplitude modulation to encode the messages that they send to the Shoredwellers. They could use various wave amplitudes to represent letters of the alphabet. For instance, a wave that is 1 millimeter higher than the carrier wave could represent the letter A, a wave that is 2 millimeters higher than the carrier wave could represent the letter B, and so on. A wave with exactly the same amplitude as the carrier wave would represent a blank space—or, alternatively, it could represent nothing at all, merely a resting space where no message is being sent. Of course, waves that are shorter than the carrier wave could also be given meaning; perhaps they could represent lowercase letters.

The chart in Figure 6 shows one possible system for encoding letters of the alphabet as wave amplitudes. The negative numbers represent waves that are taller than the carrier wave, while the positive numbers are waves that are shorter than the carrier wave. Using this system, we could encode the phrase "Hi Shoredwellers" as the following wave amplitudes:

$$8 \; -9 \; 0 \; 19 \; -8 \; -15 \; -18 \; -5 \; -4 \; -23 \; -5 \; -12$$
$$-12 \; -5 \; -18 \; -19$$

In the same way, changes in frequency (frequency modulation) or changes in degree of phase (phase modulation) could be used to encode letters of the alphabet. You might want to work out similar charts that represent the alphabet in this manner.

You'll notice that our system allows the Lakedwellers to encode all of the letters of the alphabet in both upper- and lowercase as wave amplitudes (or whatever), but that it doesn't allow them to encode punctuation marks such as periods, commas, quotation marks, etc. Of course, the Lakedwellers can work around this deficiency using words, such as *stop*, in place of punctuation marks, as in old telegrams. Or they could expand the system so that additional wave amplitudes would represent punctuation marks.

But what if the system won't expand any further? What if the water wheel used by the Lakedwellers won't produce waves that are more than 26 millimeters taller or shorter than the carrier wave?

The fact is, no matter what kind of coding system we use to encode information as a physical phenomenon such as a wave, we are going to have only a limited range of code values to use. The limited range may be very large, but it will still be limited. The range of values that can be used to encode information in a communications medium is called the *bandwidth* of the medium.

We can say, for instance, that the Lakedwellers' system of amplitude modulation codes has a bandwidth of 52 millimeters, because that's the range from the smallest amplitude to the largest amplitude that the water wheel will produce.

We can make this bandwidth more useful by using *half*-millimeter measurements to encode letters of the alphabet and punctuation marks. That would double the number of amplitudes available to use as codes. But what if the instruments being used by the Shoredwellers to measure the amplitudes aren't sensitive enough to detect half-millimeter changes in amplitude? Or if the Lakedwellers aren't skillful enough to produce changes that small? There will always be a limit to how many meaningful, detectable changes we can squeeze into a limited bandwidth, though this number will go up as our (and the Lakedweller's) instruments improve.

Another problem that the Lakedwellers will run into is *noise*. Suppose a fish jumps in the lake and creates waves of its own, or a passing boat generates a wave. These waves will get mixed up in the wave being generated by the Lakedwellers. The amplitude of these extraneous waves will add to the amplitude of the Lakedweller's wave, causing errors when the Shoredwellers try to decode it. When this happens we say that noise has been introduced into the signal.

Before we talk more about waves, however, let's talk about something else that is important for the communication of long distance messages: electricity.

2
COMMUNICATING BY WIRE

Rivers flow constantly downhill, until they reach the sea. In fact, the water in a typical river flows so constantly and so endlessly that you might find yourself asking: Where does all that water come from? Why doesn't it ever run out?

The answer is that the sun evaporates the water that flows into the sea and moves it back to the other end of the river in the form of rain. Rainwater runoff fills the river and gravity pulls it back downhill. In this way the river keeps flowing, seemingly forever. In a sense, you can think of rivers as flowing in a circle, with one half of the circle being in the riverbed and the other half in the air, where the evaporated water uses the energy of the sun to make its way back uphill.

Electricity, the stuff that runs through the electric wires strung along the highway and sticking out of the backs of table lamps, is like a river. This, in fact, is why we refer to flowing electricity as an *electric current*, by analogy to a water current. But instead of being made out of water, the river of electricity is made out of *electrons*, the infinitesimally small particles that are one of the fundamental building blocks of all matter. Electrons flow through substances known as *electrical conductors*, which have a microscopic structure that allows for the flow of electrons in much the same way that the structure of a river bed allows for the flow of water.

The river of electricity can also flow in a circle—or, literally, a *circuit*. By taking an electrically conducting substance—a metal such as copper, say—and molding it into a thin wire, we can bend the wire back into a full circle, creating a circular path for electrons to travel in.

Then, by placing an electrically operated device somewhere in the middle of that circuit of wire, we can use the energy in the moving electrons to perform work: running a motor, for instance, or lighting the filament of an incandescent bulb. Of course, this robs energy from the river of electrons, so we must place a battery or electrical generator at some other point in the circuit, to pump energy back into the electron current the way that the sun pumps energy back into a river through evaporation. To allow us to turn the device on and off, we can put a switch at yet another point in the circuit. A typical switch has two positions: on and off. When on, the current flows right through the switch and performs work. When off, the circuit is broken and the current can no longer flow.

Electrical circuits are everywhere these days. If you are indoors as you read this book, you can probably look around you and see the wires that carry electricity to and from such electrically operated devices as televisions, radios, lamps, refrigerators, microwave ovens, home computers, video game consoles, and so on. Just finding and naming all of the electrical devices, plugged and unplugged, in your home could take you all day. If you are outdoors, you are probably surrounded by electric wires traveling either above ground or underground. Even automobiles contain electrical systems run by batteries, which keep the headlights and the electronic ignition in working order.

An electric circuit, if properly designed, can carry electrons quite a long way. And, like waves, electrons can be made to carry information. When the early designers of long-distance communications systems turned to electricity to carry their messages, the field of electronic telecommunications was born.

PULSES OF INFORMATION

Information, as we have said repeatedly, involves change. The easiest way to change an electric current is to turn it on and off. By placing a switch in an electrical circuit, we can switch the current on and off in a prearranged pattern and send messages to someone at another point in the circuit. Such on/off electrical signals are commonly referred to as *pulses*.

For instance, you could string an electrical circuit between your bedroom and the bedroom of a friend in another house. Throwing a switch on and off in your bedroom could cause a small light to go on and off in your friend's bedroom. You could then send messages by turning the switch on and off once for the letter *A*, twice for the letter *B*, three times for the letter *C*, and so on, pausing briefly between letters and for a longer time between words. If there was another switch on the part of the circuit in your friend's bedroom, he or she could reply to your messages, blinking a second light bulb in your room. You'd have to be careful not to "talk" at the same time, of course.

One problem with this system is that letters that come later in the alphabet, such as the common letters *R*, *S*, *T*, and *W*, would require turning the switch on and off a ridiculously large number of times. The letter *W*, for instance, would require twenty-three separate pulses, enough to give you a sore switching finger. There are several solutions to this problem, however, as we will see.

The point of this example is that even a simple electrical circuit with two switches and two light bulbs in it can be used to carry information over a distance. Yet it took inventors more than a century to develop the first practical system of electric communication. To be fair, they were working at a handicap: theories of electricity had not yet been worked out and electrical devices such as the light bulb had not yet been invented.

THE INVENTION OF THE TELEGRAPH

The word *telegraph* means "writing at a distance." Originally, in the late eighteenth century, it referred to a system of *optical-relay semaphores*, where messengers standing on a high tower or mountaintop would use a bright light to flash messages to messengers standing on another high tower or mountaintop, who would in turn relay the message to other messengers standing on a high tower or mountaintop, and so forth. But today we use the term *telegraph* specifically to mean *electrical telegraphy*—writing at a distance with electricity.

The search for the electrical telegraph began in the early eighteenth century, about the same time that brave (and occasionally foolhardy) research-

One of Samuel F. B. Morse's early
telegraph instruments (1837)

ers had begun exploring the properties of electricity itself. (You probably recall the story of how Benjamin Franklin, the great American inventor and patriot, flew a kite in a rainstorm to study the electrical properties of lightning, thus risking his own electrocution. Unlike many such stories of our founding fathers, that one happens to be true.)

In 1727, a British experimenter transmitted a signal over an electrically charged thread one-sixth of a mile long. In 1752, an anonymous Scottish theoretician wrote a letter to a magazine proposing a communications system that would have used twenty-six electric wires, each of which could move a light ball representing a letter of the alphabet. And in 1777 the well-known Italian electrical researcher Alessandro Volta (from whose name we get the term *volt*, representing the strength of an electrical current) suggested stringing iron wires on posts to carry messages between two towns in Italy.

The modern age of electrical communications began, however, in 1832, when a struggling American portrait painter named Samuel F. B. Morse traveled to Europe and heard rumors of the electrical experimentation going on there. On the voyage home, he began sketching ideas for the communications system that eventually became the electric telegraph.

The invention he had in mind was simple: a switch would be used to open and close an electric circuit; the receiving device at the other end would use an electromagnet, powered by the electric current in the circuit, to raise and lower a pen which would make marks on a moving strip of paper. These marks would be the message sent by the telegraph.

After further thought, though, he decided that the electric current should also make audible sounds at the other end, which would also carry the message and would be understandable to a trained operator. And instead of a crude switch, he would use a key that could be pressed up and down to send the message. Finally, he began developing a code that used combinations of dots (short pulses of electric current) and dashes (longer pulses of electric current) to represent the letters of the alphabet. In time, this became the well-known Morse code, as shown in Figure 7. By combining dots and dashes in this manner, he avoided the problem of the ridiculously long sequences of pulses that we described earlier in this chapter.

One of the major problems encountered by Morse in actually building his proposed telegraph—indeed, it was a problem encountered by many of the early experimenters in telecommuni-

MORSE CODE		
A •—	J •———	S •••
B —•••	K —•—	T —
C —•—•	L •—••	U ••—
D —••	M ——	V •••—
E •	N —•	W •——
F ••—•	O ———	X —••—
G ——•	P •——•	Y —•——
H ••••	Q ——•—	Z ——••
I ••	R •—•	
1 •————	5 •••••	9 ————•
2 ••———	6 —••••	0 —————
3 •••——	7 ——•••	Period •—•—•—
4 ••••—	8 ———••	Comma ——••——

Figure 7. The Morse code.

cations—was making the electrical signal travel far enough. Electrons tend to lose energy as they travel, and the message that they carry grows weaker with distance. The first working telegraph built by Morse worked over a distance of only forty feet, hardly practical for telecommunications. But by studying more advanced electrical theory and building more and more powerful electrical generators, Morse was soon sending messages up to ten miles away. And by developing a system of relays, with one electrical signal operating a distant electromagnet that in turn sent another electrical signal that in turn operated another distant electromagnet, Morse was able to send telegraph messages over greater and greater distances.

In 1843, Morse strung the first commercial telegraph lines between the cities of Baltimore, Maryland, and Washington, D.C., a distance of 37 miles (60 km), using funds supplied by both private investors and the U.S. government. On May 24, 1844, he transmitted the first official message on the lines: "What hath God wrought?"

Samuel Morse's telegraph system came along at almost precisely the right moment in United States history. What had formerly been a relatively small nation based mostly along the east coast of the American continent had now begun a massive push to the west, with settlers spreading as far afield as California. Conventional methods of long distance communication such as mail were becoming inadequate. Stopgap measures such as the Pony Express had started to spring up, but they could only carry a limited number of messages and were far from instantaneous.

For this and other reasons, the telegraph proved immensely popular, both in the United States and elsewhere. Thousands of miles of telegraph lines were soon strung from one coast of the American continent to the other, frequently following railroad lines. The most successful of the companies stringing these wires across the nation was the Western Union Telegraph Company, a name that remains synonymous with telegraph to this day. In fact, by the early twentieth century, Western Union was officially made the *only* telegraph company in the United States, which avoided duplication of the expensive wiring and equipment that carried telegraph messages across the country.

Telegraphy was particularly popular with the press. Reporters would use the telegraph to send stories almost instantaneously to their newspapers, revolutionizing the way in which news was communicated, a revolution that continues to this day in such media as radio, television, and computer communications.

NEW KINDS OF TELEGRAPH

Dozens of inventors, including the young Thomas Edison, hastened to improve on Morse's invention, eager as they were to cash in on the popularity of the device. They developed *duplex* telegraphs (which could send messages simultaneously in both directions), *diplex* telegraphs (which could send two messages simultaneously in the *same* direction), and *quadruplex* telegraphs (which could send two messages simultaneously in both directions, for a total of four messages at one time).

Charles Wheatstone, a British inventor who was a major competitor of Morse's, invented a paper tape system that allowed messages to be recorded as a series of punched holes on a continuous strip of paper, then transmitted over telegraph lines by a machine that can read the message in the holes.

The facsimile (fax) machine transmits
a digitized image of a document via
phone lines. This new technology has
in large part supplanted the telex.

This greatly increased the speed at which messages could be sent over valuable telegraph lines.

The modern descendants of the telegraph are the *teleprinter* (sometimes incorrectly called the Teletype, which is actually a registered trademark for a popular brand of teleprinter) and the *telex* or *TWX*. Both allow telegraph messages to be typed on a standard telegraph keyboard and sent over high-speed transmission lines, to be printed out typewriter style on the other end. Even these high-speed systems, however, send information at a relatively slow rate by today's standards. More recently, however, these devices have been eclipsed by the immense popularity of *facsimile* (or *fax*) *machines*.

The fax, however, is an extension of another method of long-distance communication: the telephone.

3
VOICES ON THE WIRE

Perhaps the greatest disadvantage of the telegraph in its original form was that only a trained operator, with a knowledge of Morse code, could use it. (The modern teleprinter devices require no knowledge of Morse code, but they still require typing skills.) This meant that the number of messages was limited not only by the number of wires available for sending those messages, but by the number of operators available. And, until the development of paper-tape reading machines, the messages could only be transmitted at the speed such an operator was capable of tapping the keys—and of understanding the messages typed by another such operator.

Even if an unlimited supply of telegraph lines and machines were available, the average person would not be able to send a message over one without the aid of a trained operator unless he or she took lessons in Morse code. And even if sending and receiving Morse code were a universal skill, it's hardly as satisfactory to send a message in this manner as it is to talk to a person directly.

How much nicer it would be, the inventors of the mid-nineteenth century thought, if it were possible to send the human voice itself over a wire. Such a *telephone*—the word means, literally, "speech at a distance"—would make telecommunications available to everyone, not just those who knew how to use Morse code.

Alexander Graham Bell was a speech teacher whose primary interest was in teaching the deaf. In 1865, at the age of 18, young Graham began to grapple with the problem of sending speech over an electric wire. He phrased the problem like this:

"If I could make a current of electricity vary in intensity precisely as the air varies in density during the production of sound, I should be able to transmit speech telegraphically."[1]

Speech is made up of *sound waves*. A sound wave rises and falls in a rhythmic pattern (like a water wave), moving outward in space from its source at a speed of more than 1,000 feet per second. What rises and falls is not the level of the air but its density. When an object (such as your vocal cords) vibrates in air, it compresses the air immediately around it. Air doesn't like to remain compressed any more than the tiny hill of water around the fallen stone in Chapter One likes to stay up in the air—and so it uncompresses, in turn compressing the air around it. In this way, the area of compressed air around the vibrating object spreads outward in an ever-growing sphere the way that the hill of water spreads out around the fallen stone.

[1]Quoted in Fox, Linda, ed., *Broadcasting & Communications*, Arco Publishing Company, New York, 1978.]

50

This region of compressed air is a sound wave. When it strikes the ear drum of a listener, it causes the drum to vibrate, in almost exactly the same pattern that the object causing the sound wave was vibrating. Mechanisms inside the ear and brain of the listener translate these vibrations into a meaningful form. If what caused the vibrations was the vocal cords of a speaker, what will be heard inside the brain of the listener will be speech. If what caused the vibrations was a musical instrument played by a skilled musician, what will be heard is music. (If the musician is not so skilled, what will be heard may be noise.)

Although sound waves are compression waves rather than the *transverse* (up and down) waves the falling stone creates in the water, we can still represent those waves as a rising and falling line. The simplest sound wave, like the simplest water wave, is just a sine wave. In real life, such simple sounds rarely occur, though the pure tone produced by a tuning fork comes close. A sound wave, in fact, has all of the properties of a water wave: crests (the points of maximum air density), troughs (the points of minimum air density), wavelength (the distance from crest to crest or trough to trough), frequency (the number of crests to pass a given point in one second), amplitude (the difference in air pressure from crest to trough), and phase (the relative position of the wave in space). When two or more simple sound waves come together, they produce a complex sound wave that is the sum of the waves.

We perceive sound waves differently from water waves, though. We perceive them as sounds inside our head. As the frequency of the sound wave increases (i.e., as the wavelength becomes shorter), the pitch of the sound goes up. As the frequency of the sound wave decreases (as the wavelength becomes longer), the pitch of the sound goes down. As the amplitude increases, the sound becomes louder. As the amplitude decreases, the sound becomes fainter. Speech is mostly a matter of frequency modulation, with a touch of amplitude and phase modulation thrown in. The changing form of the sound wave carries the information in the speech, just as the changing amplitudes of water waves carry the messages sent from the Lakedwellers to the Shoredwellers (see Chapter One). Complex mechanisms in our head measure and decode these changes and present them to us in a highly processed form that doesn't actually seem much like a wave, but is one nonetheless.

When Alexander Graham Bell suggested making a "current of electricity vary in intensity precisely as the air varies in density," he was proposing one of the most important ideas in all of telecommunications: the idea of *analog information transmission*. The word analog refers to something that is like something else—that is *analogous* to something else—in a certain way. Analog information transmission, then, involves finding something that is like the information that you wish to transmit—that is, something that is an analog of that information—but that travels over long distances more efficiently than the form normally taken by that information. To the inventor of the telephone, that meant turning an electric current into an analog of a sound wave.

Bell realized that by making the intensity, or strength, of an electric current rise and fall exactly as a sound wave rises and falls (that is, increases and decreases in density), the electric current becomes an analog of the sound wave. If transmitted over a circuit, a device at another point in the cir-

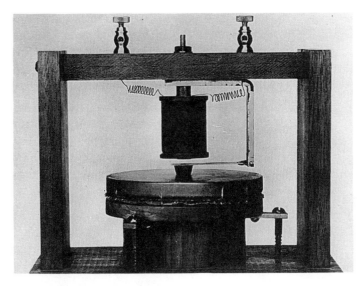

Model of Bell's first telephone.
He transmitted sounds electrically
through this device in 1875.

cuit could be used to translate the analog electric
signal back into a real sound wave, reproducing
the sound at a distance.

But turning an electric current into an imita-
tion sound wave is a little more difficult than just
turning the current on and off. Something a little
more complicated than a switch would be needed
to send the message. It required what we now refer to as a *microphone* and a *speaker*.

The principle of the microphone is fairly simple, if not as simple as that of an electric switch.
Some electrical conductors conduct electricity
better than others. To make a microphone, you need
a substance that conducts electricity better when
it's being squeezed than when it's not being

squeezed; a collection of carbon particles will do the trick. You then place a diaphragm (a flat membrane that will vibrate when sound waves strike it) next to the conductor so that vibrations in the diaphragm will squeeze the conductor and change its electrical conductivity.

In this way, the sound waves striking the diaphragm (and thereby squeezing the conductor) will change the strength of the electric current passing through the conductor in exactly the same pattern as the changing density of the air waves. A wave crest will push the diaphragm against the conductor, squeezing it and causing the electric current to increase in intensity. A wave trough will "pull" against the diaphragm, unsqueezing the conductor and causing the electric current to decrease in intensity.

The speaker, at the other end of the electric circuit from the microphone, reverses this process. The rising and falling electric current transmitted on the circuit powers an electromagnet, which causes a second diaphragm to move out and in as the electric current increases and decreases. This vibrating diaphragm produces a sound wave, which is nearly identical to the one striking the microphone. In this way, the sound wave striking the microphone can be transmitted as far as an electric current can be carried, which in Bell's time meant as far as a telegraph message would go. That, at least, was the theory.

Most of the ideas and pieces needed for the invention of the telephone were available by the time Bell came along; it was his genius to put them together into a working telephone that was also a commercially practical invention. On March 10, 1876, while experimenting with a telephone apparatus, Bell spilled acid on his clothing and called for his assistant with the famous words: "Mr. Watson, come here, I want you." Watson, who was on a different floor of the building at the time, heard the inventor's cry over the telephone, marking the first voice message ever sent over wires.

Bell's telephone was the hit of the 1876 Centennial Exposition in Philadelphia. Emperor Pedro II of Brazil dropped a demonstration telephone in astonishment, exclaiming "It talks!" The telephone caught on almost immediately in both the United States and England. No less an inventor than Thomas Edison was inspired to develop a better microphone than the one used by Bell. (The microphone described earlier is actually closer to the one invented by Edison than the original, cruder model used by Bell.)

Sensing the commercial potential of the device, Bell founded the Bell Telephone Company. Worried that they would face competition from the powerful Western Union corporation, which had already placed electric communication lines across much of the United States, Bell arrived at an agreement with that corporation by promising not to become involved in the telegraph business while Western Union promised to stay out of the telephone business.

THE TELEPHONE SYSTEM

One of the thorniest problems facing the early telephone operators was how to connect a caller with the person being called. Many early systems were party lines, with an entire community constantly interconnected on what amounted to a single telephone line. When someone wanted to make a call, they turned a crank in a specified pattern, causing a ringing noise on all the other phones in the community. The person whose ringing pattern had been invoked would then answer the call—but anyone else who wanted to could also answer the phone or eavesdrop on the call (and they frequently did). Such systems were still in place in rural communities into the middle of the twentieth century.

An early solution to the problem of making phone calls private was the *manual switchboard*. With this system, all telephones within a community were connected to a central operator, who sat in front of a large board with sockets for all of the telephones lines in the community. A caller would tell the operator which other individual in the community they wished to speak with and the operator would use a small electric cord with plugs on both ends to connect the caller's socket with the socket of the telephone line they wished to call. The recipient's telephone, now connected directly to the caller's telephone, would ring and the call could go through—assuming the recipient was home at the time. Imagine, however, the problem in a city like New York, where 10,000 lines came together in one large central office circa 1890. To solve the problem of manual switching, the so-called *crossbar systems* were developed to automate the switchboard process by using an electromechanical device to connect one telephone line to another. They came as a result of the invention of the Strowger switch by Almon Strowger in 1889.

Currently, this process is done electronically, in some cases using special-purpose computers programmed to route calls through complex networks of electronic circuits. In Chapter Six, we'll see how the telephone systems of the near future will be so thoroughly computerized that they will even treat the telephone calls themselves as computer data.

LONG DISTANCE

Early telephone systems were entirely local and were capable of connecting those on the system with others on the same system—but not with users of other systems. This meant, in effect, that you could call your neighbors in the same town but that you couldn't call family, friend, and business associates in another town. This kept the telegraph companies and the post office happy, but it severely limited telephone use.

A telephone signal is more complex than the simple on-off pulses of a telegraph signal. Not only did the signal become weaker with distance, but it became distorted, the voice and words eventually unrecognizable. It was necessary to find newer ways of relaying a signal over long distances than those used for the telegraph.

Part of the problem was that early telephone and telegraph circuits used the earth itself as part of the circuit. The flow of electricity would travel through the wire in one direction, then return to the source through the ground. Such ground signals were subject to various types of noise, including interference from other signals returning through the same ground. The solution was to use two wires for each circuit, often twisted about each other in a double-spiral. (Such double wires are sometimes called *twisted-pair wires*.)

Other solutions were eventually found to minimize such interference and distortion. (This is not to say that the problems have been completely solved. Anyone who has used a telephone is familiar with the strange sounds and noises that can invade the silent moments of an otherwise clear conversation. In Chapter Six, we'll see how this problem may finally be cured by the transition from the current analog telephone technology, based on Bell's notion of varying the intensity of the electric signal in the same pattern as a sound wave, to more up-to-date digital technology, which transmits telephone conversations as computer data.) Still, another problem remained: amplification.

An amplifier takes an electrical signal carrying information and makes it stronger. If the information that the signal carries is sound, then the effect is to make it louder, which is what we normally think of when we hear the term *amplification*. The way most modern amplifiers work is this: the electrical current to be amplified is run through a special circuit where it controls a stronger electric current. As the original, weaker current increases in intensity, so does the stronger current. As the original current decreases in intensity, so does the stronger current. In this way, the information in the weaker current is transferred to the stronger current, in a considerably magnified form. Although it is the weaker signal that enters the amplifier, it is the stronger signal that leaves it.

The first practical amplifier was developed in 1906 by the American inventor Lee de Forest. It was based on a vacuum tube and became the basis, in one form or another, for most of the telecommunications technology that followed in the first half of the twentieth century. In the late 1940s, a new method of amplification and control of electronic signals was developed, based on so-called *semiconducting materials*. They were called *transistors* and they revolutionized communications technology—and all other forms of information

The first transistor
ever assembled (1947).
It was made of germanium,
a semiconducting material.

These three Bell Labs
scientists shared the
Nobel Prize for Physics in
1956 for the invention
of the transistor. Left
to right: John Bardeen,
William Shockley, and
Walter H. Brattain.

processing technology—by allowing sophisticated electronic circuits to be made smaller and cooler and therefore less unwieldy and more portable.

The development of amplifiers allowed long-distance calls to be sent anywhere—and indeed it is possible today to make a long-distance call to almost any place in the world. Transatlantic cables laid beneath the Atlantic Ocean in 1956 made it possible for phone calls to cross between continents. Today, telephone calls are carried by more than just cables. They are transferred from one microwave relay station to another and even bounced off satellites, techniques that marry telephone technology with the radio technology to be discussed in the next chapter.

The telephone was the first device to allow transmission of the human voice and other sounds over long distances—eventually, around the world. But it was not the last such device. In fact, a quarter of a century after Bell called to his assistant over the first telephone, an Italian inventor built a device that was destined to carry the human voice to places where telephones could never go, even through the depths of space itself.

4
COMMUNICATION THROUGH SPACE

The telephone and telegraph could transmit information at nearly instantaneous speeds to anywhere that a wire could go. But it was the wire that was both the strength and weakness of these media. Run a wire from the north to the south pole and you could send a message between the ends of the earth. But there were places to which wires simply could not go.

One of these was the middle of the ocean. The transatlantic cable traveled beneath the ocean, jumping from continent to continent, but there was no way that a ship could tap into the wire to pick up a message. Travelers in the middle of the sea, along with people who lived on obscure islands or distant segments of continents not worth running cables to, were cut off from the worldwide grid of telecommunications. What was needed to bring them into the fold was some sort of *wireless* method of electronic communications.

When wireless telecommunication finally arrived at the beginning of the twentieth century, it was seen as a means of sending messages to and from ships at sea, a worthy but hardly earthshaking goal. But within two decades, this new technology had given birth to a brand-new *form* of communication, one not quite like any form of communication previously known. That new form was called *broadcasting*.

THE ELECTROMAGNETIC SPECTRUM

In the middle of the nineteenth century, the great English physicist James Clerk Maxwell discovered a new kind of wave (though upon studying it carefully he realized that it had in fact been known for a very long time indeed). Maxwell discovered that when a wire or other conductor with an electric current moving through it is moved back and forth rapidly, it produces a magnetic field around itself (like the field of force around a magnet), which in turn produces an electrically charged field around itself, which in turn produces another magnetic field around itself, and so forth. This alternating electric-magnetic field spreads out rapidly from its source in the same way that a sound wave radiates outward from a vibrating object.

He dubbed this new type of wave *electromagnetic radiation*. When he calculated its properties he realized that they were identical to the properties of another, well-known type of radiation: light. Therefore, Maxwell reasoned, light must be a form of electromagnetic radiation.

Electromagnetic radiation has all of the essential attributes of a wave: frequency, wavelength, amplitude, phase, and so forth. And while water waves travel through water and sound waves through air, the medium that electromagnetic radiation traveled through was space itself, empty space. (It was not immediately understood that waves could travel through space the same way that they travel through more seemingly substantial media such as water and air. So until the early twentieth century it was assumed that there was an invisible substance pervading space through which the electromagnetic waves traveled. This substance was dubbed the *luminiferous* ("light-carrying") *ether*. Today we know that the luminiferous ether does not exist.)

But the phenomenon that we call light (or, more properly, "visible light") is only one type of electromagnetic radiation. Specifically, it is electromagnetic radiation with a frequency of between 10,000 and 100,000 GHz. (GHz stands for "giga-Hertz," or 1 billion cycles per second.) Lower frequency light waves with frequencies near 10,000 GHz are blue in color, while high-frequency light waves with frequencies near 100,000 GHz are red in color. The other colors of the rainbow have frequencies in between these two extremes. In fact, when you see a rainbow you are seeing light waves sorted into the order of their frequencies by the prismatic effect of raindrops.

There are also forms of electromagnetic radiation that you cannot see with your eyes. In fact, most wavelengths of electromagnetic radiation are quite invisible. Just below the frequency of blue light, for instance, comes the appropriately named ultraviolet radiation. And just above the frequency of red light comes infrared rays. The chart in Figure 8 reveals that still other wavelengths of electromagnetic radiation take the form of gamma rays, cosmic rays, X rays—and radio waves.

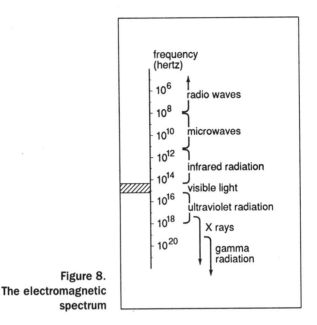

frequency
(hertz)

10^6 radio waves

10^8

10^{10} microwaves

10^{12}

infrared radiation

10^{14}

visible light

10^{16}

ultraviolet radiation

10^{18}

X rays

10^{20}

gamma
radiation

Figure 8.
The electromagnetic
spectrum

MARCONI AND THE RADIO

The importance of Maxwell's discovery was not lost on the inventors of the late nineteenth century. If electromagnetic radiation can travel great distances through empty space—and light, as we know, can travel trillions of trillions of miles, all the way from distant stars, galaxies, and quasars—then it was the ideal medium for carrying information literally anywhere. If a message could be encoded in an electromagnetic wave, and decoded at its destination, then that message could go anywhere that light could go. In fact, it could go further, because some forms of electromagnetic radiation can penetrate matter itself.

What was needed was a method of reliably generating an electromagnetic wave on demand, plus a way to make that wave travel over long distances without becoming too weak to detect—and a way to modulate the amplitude, frequency or phase of that wave so that it could carry information. The first problem was solved in 1888 by the German physicist Heinrich Hertz, in whose honor we use the term Hertz to denote the frequency of a wave.

Hertz constructed an electric circuit with a gap in it, then ran an alternating electric current through it. (An *alternating current*—usually abbreviated AC—is a current that runs in one direction around the circuit for a fraction of a second then reverses direction and runs in the other direction for another fraction of a second, rather like a river that can go into reverse.) As the current reached its peak strength in each direction, it would build up such a powerful electric charge that the current would leap across the gap, called a *spark gap*, to complete the circuit. The spark created a powerful burst of electromagnetic radiation.

The type of electromagnetic radiation produced by Hertz was dubbed "Hertzian waves" at the time. But soon it would have another name: radio.

Hertz's experiments caught the imagination of a teenaged Italian inventor named Guglielmo Marconi. The young Marconi, the son of wealthy parents, lived on a large estate, where he experimented with spark gap transmitters. Soon he could send short bursts of Hertzian waves more than two miles, where they could be detected by a crude receiver. He also had the inspiration to attach a telegraph key to the transmitter, so that he could turn the spark gap on and off in discrete pulses—and send messages in Morse code.

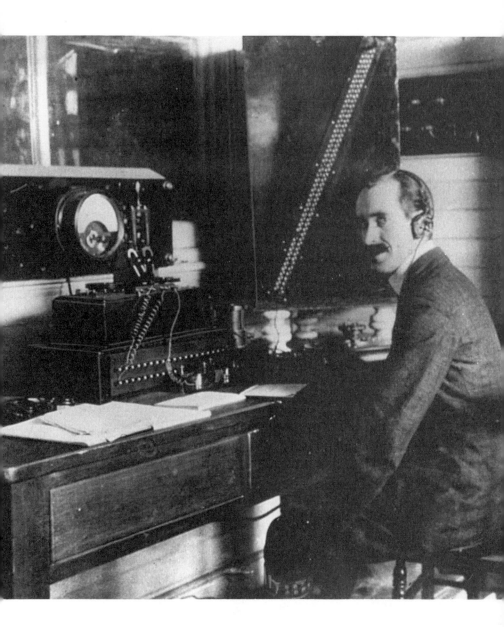

Guglielmo Marconi (1874–1937), with
the wireless telegraph he invented

In 1896, Marconi's mother (who was British by birth) took him to England, where he gained the support of William Preece, the head telegrapher of the British Post Office. Under Preece's guidance, by 1899 Marconi was sending electromagnetic signals all the way across the English Channel. Finally, in 1901, he sent a message across the Atlantic Ocean, from England to Newfoundland. It consisted of the Morse code for the letter *S*.

What Marconi had invented was *wireless telegraphy* ("wireless," for short)—or, later, *radiotelegraphy*. It was immediately seized on as a method of sending messages between ships at sea, or from ship to shore and shore to ship. In 1912, for instance, the crew of the luxury liner H.M.S. *Titanic* used a wireless transmitter to send a distress signal after the supposedly unsinkable ship was struck by an iceberg. Marconi himself used his wireless devices for reporting the results of yacht races while the races were still in progress, thus garnering invaluable publicity for his invention, publicity that no doubt stoked the success of his new company British Marconi.

Although radio waves are used to this day for transmitting coded messages at high speeds, we don't usually think of radio as a medium for telegraph-style transmission. Rather, we think of it as a medium for transmitting sound, particularly voice and music. The debut of *radiotelephony*—the use of radio to send telephone-style messages over the "airwaves"—came in 1906, when the Canadian-American physicist Reginald Fessenden used amplitude modulation to encode a sound wave on a radio wave and broadcast the results to a surprised audience of radiotelegraphers along the East Coast of the United States.

AM RADIO

How can you use amplitude modulation to encode a sound wave on a radio wave? The principle is simple, as illustrated in Figure 9. The first part of the illustration, Figure 9a, shows a sinelike carrier wave. Imagine that this is the electromagnetic wave that we are going to use to carry sound. Figure 9b shows the complex sound wave that we are going to encode on the carrier wave. It rises and falls in a pattern completely different from that of the carrier wave.

Finally, Figure 9c shows the carrier wave after it has been amplitude modulated to carry the sound wave. The wave *crests* of the carrier wave rise and fall just as the sound wave itself rises and falls. In other words, the amplitude of the carrier waves has become an analog of the sound wave. Thus, this is a form of analog information transmission.

The process of physically modulating the carrier wave is not unlike the process of modulating the electric current in a telephone system. A microphone is used to create a rising and falling electric analog of a sound wave. This electric current is in turn used to boost the energy that produces the carrier wave, making it more intense (increasing its amplitude) as the sound wave rises, making it less intense (decreasing its amplitude) as the sound wave falls.

Unlike the spark gap transmitters used by Marconi, the transmitter used for AM radio produces a constant electromagnetic signal at a constant frequency. And, just as an electric current moving through a conductor can create an electromagnetic signal, this signal can in turn create an electric current (albeit a weak one) in an electrical conductor. A conductor designed to carry an elec-

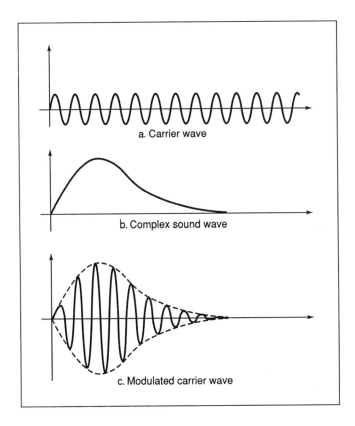

a. Carrier wave

b. Complex sound wave

c. Modulated carrier wave

**Figure 9. How AM radio broadcasts.
The complex sound wave modulates
the amplitude of the carrier wave.**

tric current created by a radio signal is called a *receiving antenna*. The electric current in the antenna is then used to operate an electromagnet which makes a speaker vibrate—similarly, once again, to the same process in a telephone.

(Although much of the process of producing and receiving a radio wave is similar to that used with the telephone, you may have noticed that radio sound is distinctly superior to telephone sound. This is because the range of sound waves in a telephone

69

is deliberately restricted to a range much smaller than that normally detected by the human ear, so that telephone signals occupy a smaller bandwidth and will not crowd the wires used to transmit them. Radio waves also have a somewhat restricted bandwidth, but the restrictions are not as great.)

Fessenden's radio broadcast of 1906 featured Fessenden himself singing, playing the violin and reading selections from the Bible. In addition, he broadcast music played on a phonograph, making Fessenden the world's first disk jockey. This marked the beginning of the phenomenon of radio (and, later, television) broadcasting.

THE BIRTH OF BROADCASTING

Radio was originally conceived as a form of *point-to-point communication*, a way of sending a message from a single source to a single recipient. In effect, it was to be telephone without the wires, hence the term *radiotelephony*. Unfortunately, radio had a serious deficiency as a point-to-point medium: anybody could listen in. As it turned out, this "deficiency" was radio's greatest advantage.

The word *broadcasting* originally meant to scatter seeds by hand. Seeds spread in this manner will sometimes fall on fallow ground and die, but a few may find fertile soil and begin to grow. In the same way, radio broadcasters were those brave individuals who send radio signals out into the airwaves without knowing whether anyone was listening or not. In the beginning, relatively few people were. But that would change.

The first broadcasters were enthusiastic amateurs who could afford to build their own transmitters and who had the time to produce "programs" consisting mostly of inconsequential chatter and improvised music. The first listeners were also enthusiastic amateurs, with homemade receivers that could detect the stray broadcasts floating across the airwaves.

If radio broadcasting were ever to progress beyond the early amateur programming of Fessenden and his followers, someone was going to have to pay for the equipment and production facilities that high-quality broadcasting would require. But there was no way to charge the audience for the privilege of listening to a radio broadcast, the way that you might charge someone for viewing a movie or watching a play. Radio broadcasts were essentially free; they went almost everywhere and could be enjoyed by anyone with a receiver.

It was necessary, therefore, to charge the broadcaster for the privilege of sending out information. Or, to be more precise, it was necessary for the broadcaster to find someone who was willing to foot the bill in exchange for adding a few messages of that person's choice to the broadcast. Thus was born radio advertising.

Advertising or no, early radio broadcasters faced a paradox familiar to pioneers in any medium. If few people were listening, then advertisers would be unwilling to invest dollars for the production or programs. But if there were no programs, few people would listen. In the words of a later generation, it was a Catch 22 situation.

This remained the state of radio broadcasting from the time of Fessenden in 1906 until the early 1920s. Then, in 1922, the situation began to change. Curious about this new medium they had been reading about, people suddenly started buying radio receivers in large numbers. In the year 1922 alone, 100,000 radios were sold. Within the course of a year, radio went from being the province of a small band of dedicated amateurs to a genuine popular phenomenon.

Where listeners went, broadcasters followed. In the year 1920, there had been thirty licensed radio stations in the United States. By spring of 1922, there were more than two hundred. With so many radio stations in one country (not to mention many more abroad), there was the threat of utter chaos on the airwaves, as stations began to interfere with one another in much the same way the waves from the two stones tossed into our still pool of water in Chapter One interfered with one another.

Fortunately, not long after the radio boom swept across America, broadcasting regulation arrived.

STATIONS AND PROGRAMMING

Early radio stations were licensed by the U.S. Department of Commerce to broadcast at a frequency of 833.2 KHz, that is, these early stations used carrier waves with frequencies of 833,200 cycles per second. Because they were all at the same frequency, only one station could broadcast in a given area at one time. This wasn't always a problem; most early stations broadcast only a few hours a day, at the discretion of their owners. But soon this situation led to conflicts between broadcasters as to who was going to be able to broadcast when.

The solution, in 1927, was the creation of a five person agency called the Federal Radio Commission (FRC). It was the job of the FRC not only to license broadcasting stations but to allocate frequencies—that is, to assign specific carrier wave frequencies to specific stations so that they could broadcast in the same area without interfering with one another. (Obviously, radio receivers had to be

An early RCA cathedral radio

redesigned so that they could be adjusted to receive a variety of radio frequencies.)

In 1934, the role of the FRC was usurped by the Federal Communications Commission (FCC), which still licenses stations and allocates frequencies today, though its role has been extended to television and other communications media.

One of the first significant radio stations was KDKA in Pittsburgh, Pennsylvania, owned by the Westinghouse Corporation. In a sense, the station itself constituted an advertisement for Westinghouse products. The company assumed that if they supported a station and paid for its programs, people would buy Westinghouse radios to listen to it. The station debuted on November 2, 1920. Opening night programming included coverage of the 1920 presidential election mixed with live banjo music.

Westinghouse, along with General Electric and RCA, founded station WJZ in New York in October of 1921. The station eventually became the flagship of a *network* of stations across the country that shared programming produced by the corporate owners. In 1926, this network was officially named the National Broadcasting Company (NBC). The next year, however, it was broken into two separate networks, the Red Network (which is still called NBC today) and the Blue Network (which eventually broke away from NBC and became the American Broadcasting Company (ABC)). WJZ was later renamed WABC.

In 1927, another radio network was formed in competition with NBC. It was originally known as the Columbia Phonograph Broadcasting System, though the name was later shortened to the Columbia Broadcasting System (CBS).

Modern broadcast programming began to take shape in the late 1920s and early 1930s. The first hit radio show, *Amos and Andy*, debuted on NBC in 1929 and introduced a new form of entertainment to American society: the situation comedy. Although its depiction of comical blacks (portrayed by white actors) living in an imaginary ghetto was racist by modern standards (and even by the standards of some contemporary critics), the immense success of the show led to a flood of imitations and assured the success of the new medium. People began to organize their lives around radio programs, much as they would later organize their lives around television programs.

Most genres of program later found on television—the situation comedy, the soap opera, the news program, the crime drama, the game show—were anticipated by radio programs. Even such cutting-edge 1980s television formats as all-news TV (CNN) and all music television (MTV) were preceded decades earlier by similar radio formats.

FM RADIO

Amplitude modulated, or AM, radio was for many years known as *standard broadcasting*, because it was the only method of broadcasting in use transmitting programs to the general public. But AM radio had its drawbacks. For one thing, the bandwidth allotted to stations by the FCC was not sufficient for a full range of sound, somewhat lowering the quality of broadcast music. More importantly, it was subject to interference from other sources of electromagnetic radiation—lightning, for instance, or sunspots—which could add their amplitudes to the AM signal and produce extraneous superwaves. These superwaves were heard by the listener as *static*.

In the 1930s, an inventor named Edwin H. Armstrong demonstrated a new method of encoding sound waves on radio waves: frequency modulation or FM. Figure 10 demonstrates Armstrong's process. As before, Figure 10a shows an unmodulated carrier wave, Figure 10b shows a sound wave to be encoded on the carrier wave, and Figure 10c shows the modulated carrier wave. Notice that when the sound wave approaches its peak, the wavelength of the carrier wave decreases (and therefore its frequency increases). When the sound wave goes down, the wavelength of the carrier wave increases (and therefore its frequency decreases). The frequency of the carrier wave now carries the sound information.

The primary advantage of FM over AM was that it was almost entirely static free. Extraneous radiation sources that added their amplitudes to the FM signal had no effect on the sound, because the receiver ignored the amplitude; only the frequency held information. But there was little immediate interest in Armstrong's invention, in part because AM was already so thoroughly entrenched. And the Catch 22 that originally dogged AM radio was once again in effect: nobody wanted to build FM stations until listeners owned FM radios but nobody wanted FM radios until there was something to listen to.

It wasn't until the 1950s that FM radio began to catch on. But by the 1970s it had far surpassed AM radio in popularity because of the superiority

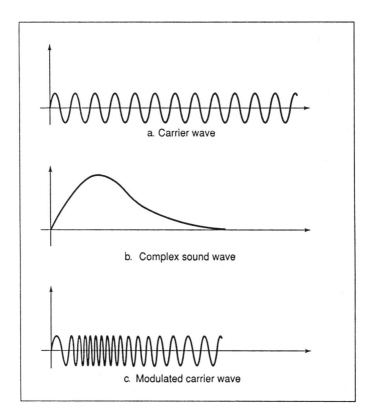

a. Carrier wave

b. Complex sound wave

c. Modulated carrier wave

Figure 10. FM radio differs from AM radio in that the complex sound wave modulates not the amplitude but rather the *frequency* of the carrier wave.

of the sound reproduction. Today, almost all popular music stations are on FM radio, while AM radio is more oriented toward talk and news programming, where sound quality is less important.

In the 1950s, radio was shaken by competition from a new medium, resulting in radical changes in radio programming. Today, instead of hearing situation comedies and soap operas on the radio, we hear music shows, talk shows, and news shows.

That new medium was, of course, television.

5
PICTURES THROUGH SPACE

Television is sometimes called "radio with pictures." Certainly early television fit this description. Like radio, television is broadcast via electromagnetic waves. Most of the early programming on television was an extension of the programming on radio. And the sound that accompanies the television picture is essentially an FM transmission.

But the problem of broadcasting pictures is much subtler and more difficult than the problems of broadcasting sound, which not only explains why televisions cost several times as much as radios of comparable quality but why it was nearly half a century from the first radio experiments to the first regularly scheduled television broadcasts.

PAINTING WITH ELECTRONS

Still, as complicated as they are, the basic principles behind television aren't difficult to under-

79

stand. You can grasp a few of them simply by looking closely at the picture on a television set.

A television picture is made up of a series of horizontal lines, stacked one above the other from the top of the screen to the bottom. These lines, called *raster lines* or *scanning lines,* appear on the inside of the glass screen of the *picture tube* or *cathode ray tube (CRT)* inside the television. They are produced by an *electron scanning gun* in the rear of the CRT that shoots a steady stream of electrons which strike a phosphor coating inside the screen. When the electrons strike the phosphors, they glow—and continue to glow for a fraction of a second.

A single stream of electrons, however, can only make the phosphors glow in a single small point of light. To create the full set of raster lines that make up the picture, a magnetic field inside the CRT pulls the electron stream from the left side to the right side (as viewed from the front) of the screen, thus painting a complete raster line across the screen. The electron gun is then turned off and the magnetic field used to reposition it back at the left side of the screen, slightly below its previous position. (This repositioning is called the *horizontal retrace.* The brief period during which it takes place is called the *horizontal blank,* because no television image is transmitted while it is happening.) Another raster line is painted and the process repeated. When the electron stream reaches the bottom right-hand corner of the picture, it is turned off again and repositioned at the upper left-hand corner of the screen. (This is called the *vertical retrace,* which takes place during the *vertical blank.*) This entire process takes one-sixtieth of a second, so it looks to the viewer as though the entire picture has appeared instantaneously.

Once this process is complete, the glowing phosphors inside the CRT hold a complete television image. (Actually, they hold *half* of a complete image, as we will explain in a moment.) But the phosphors will begin to lose their glow in a little more than a sixtieth of a second and the image will begin to flicker and fade. So the process has to be repeated sixty times a second to maintain a constant image.

The preceding explanation tells us how the raster lines get drawn on the television screen, but it doesn't tell us how those lines form an image. A continuous stream of electrons would paint a pure white picture on the television screen, which would be rather boring. Television is interesting precisely because the raster lines produced by the electron gun are capable of carrying a picture. But where does that picture come from?

First let's examine the process of creating a black-and-white television picture, since that is substantially simpler than the process of creating a color picture. This process begins in a television camera. Light from the scene being photographed enters a lens, as it does in a still camera or movie camera. But instead of being focused on chemically treated film, the image is focused on a metal plate. This so-called *target plate*, located inside the camera's *pickup tube*, is covered with a light-sensitive substance that converts the energy of the light striking it into electricity. This electricity remains stored inside the plate itself, with greater amounts of electricity where the plate is being struck by bright light and lesser amounts of electricity where the plate is being struck by dimmer light. In a sense, the electric charge on the plate is now an analog of the image being focused on it.

An electron gun, similar to that used in a television, scans across the rear of the plate line by line the same way the electron gun in a television scans across the inside of the picture tube. Wherever the electron stream hits the target plate it releases the electricity stored in that part of the plate. The electric current then flows out of the plate and into circuits attached to the plate. Because the electricity stored in any part of the plate is equivalent to the amount of light striking that part, the electric current leaving the plate is also an analog of the image on the plate—except that now the image has been broken up into a series of scanning lines, as the electron beam scans across the rear of the plate.

This electron current is used to produce an amplitude-modulated electromagnetic signal, that is, an electromagnetic signal that rises in amplitude to represent the bright parts of the picture and falls in amplitude to represent the dark parts. This signal is broadcast over the airwaves, where it is detected by television antennas and converted back to an electric current. The current is amplified and used to power the stream of electrons leaving the electron gun in the television's picture tube. Now the stream of electrons increases in intensity to represent the bright parts of the image and decreases in intensity to represent the dark parts of the image. Because it is the intensity of the electron stream that determines how brightly the phosphors inside the picture tube glow, what appears on the inside of the picture tube looks to our eyes like a black-and-white reproduction of the image being photographed inside the TV studio.

Even disregarding the fact that the image we have described is black and white, it is by no means identical to the image being focused on the target plate. For one thing, it is broken up into lines, while the image on the plate is continuous across the surface of the plate. Also, the image on the TV screen is only updated every sixtieth of a second, while the image on the target plate is constantly changing. In both cases, it is our own eyes that give us the illusion of a complete, constantly moving image. If we sit back far enough from the television screen, we scarcely notice that it is broken up into lines and we see it as continuous, even if the image isn't truly continuous. And the sixtieth of a second updates arrive so quickly on the screen that to our eyes they give the illusion of constant motion, even if what we are actually seeing is a series of still frames one after another.

Actually, as we alluded earlier, the picture isn't completely updated every sixtieth of a second; only half of the picture is updated. The reason for this is that it requires one-thirtieth of a second to transmit an entire television picture, but the phosphors on the inside of the picture tube will begin to lose their glow in a little more than a sixtieth of a second. If the electron gun scanned a picture in one-thirtieth of a second, as would seem to be required, the phosphors at the top of the screen would begin to darken while the raster lines at the bottom of the screen were still being drawn (and vice versa). This would produce an annoying flicker that would look distinctly unappealing to the viewer.

The solution is *interlace*. Every sixtieth of a second, the television station transmits every other line of the picture. First it transmits the even numbered lines, then in the next sixtieth of a second it transmits the odd numbered lines. Thus the entire television screen (and all of the phosphors) can be *refreshed* every sixtieth of a second to prevent flicker, but it still takes one-thirtieth of a second to send the entire picture.

To add color to a picture, the television camera must create four separate pictures, one for each of the primary colors of light (red, yellow, green, and blue) plus a black-and-white image. In some cases, this is done by having four separate pickup tubes in the camera, one for each of these colors. The three color images are combined to form a so-called *chrominance signal*, which is broadcast at a slightly different frequency than the black-and-white, or *luminance*, signal. The process by which all of this achieved is somewhat more complex than we have space to describe here; the For Further Reading section at the end of this book lists several other books that explain the process in more detail.

A color television uses red, green, and blue phosphor dots on the inside of the picture tube; you can see these dots if you look closely at a television screen. The electron scanning gun is carefully aimed at the appropriate dots to produce a properly colored picture. The viewer's eye then mixes the light it receives in each of these colors to form the actual color of that part of the image. Because each dot (or *pixel*, short for "pictorial element") of a color television picture is made up of three phosphor dots, a color image contains less detail than a black and white image. Thus, the black-and-white, or luminance, signal is used by a color television to produce the fine detail in the picture.

The specifics of the television signal used in the United States and Japan are slightly different from the specifics of the television signal used in Europe and much of the rest of the world. The U.S. system is called the *NTSC* (for *National Television System*

Committee, the organization that formulated the standard) system. The NTSC system, which is essentially the one we have described above, transmits a picture consisting of 525 interlaced lines updated 30 times per second, while the European PAL *(phase alternating line)* system transmits a picture consisting of 625 interlaced lines updated 25 times a second. The European picture is slightly more detailed, but uses fewer frames per second than the American system.

THE DEVELOPMENT OF TELEVISION

Surprisingly, inventors were working on television systems even before the invention of radio. The German inventor Paul Nipkow patented a television system in 1884. It used a rotating disk with small holes drilled through it in a spiral pattern. Light from the image to be televised would shine through the holes and strike a photoelectric cell that would convert the light into an electric current. As in modern television systems, bright light would produce a stronger electric current than dimmer light and the overall current would become an analog of the image being photographed. A similar disk would reproduce the image by rotating in front of a lamp that would brighten and dim as the electric current rose and fell. A viewer standing in front of the disk would perceive the illusion of a television picture scanned out by the rotating holes on the disk. Because electromagnetic waves had not been harnessed yet for broadcast purposes, this system would have required images to be transmitted by wire, not unlike modern cable television systems.

The so-called Nipkow disk was the basis for most early television systems. In 1908, however, a

Scottish engineer named A. A. Campbell Swinton suggested using a cathode ray tube (which had been invented by physicists a decade earlier and used to study the newly discovered electron) and a magnetic field to scan out a television image. But most inventors persisted working with Nipkow-style disks through the 1920s.

It wasn't until 1932 that RCA demonstrated a working CRT-based television. In 1939, an essentially modern television system was demonstrated at the New York World's Fair (though the first working television broadcasts, using a much cruder system, had begun in Germany in 1935). World War II intervened, however, and regular television broadcasting did not begin until the late 1940s. The three major radio networks all developed television subsidiaries, which eventually eclipsed their radio counterparts.

Modern color television was developed in the late 1930s and early 1940s, but was not adopted by U.S. television until 1954. Most shows in those days were black and white. Early color programming was primarily on NBC, with ABC adding a few color shows to its schedule in the early 1960s. Then, in 1965, NBC announced that all of the shows on its fall schedule (with two exceptions) would be in color and the other two networks beefed up their color programming in response. By the fall of 1966, all network television programming in the United States (with the exception of reruns of older programs and some movies) was in color. In the mid-1980s, stereo sound was added to some television broadcasts, and has become a growing trend.

Early television programs were broadcast either live or on film. There was no way to preserve live programming for posterity other than filming the image directly off a studio monitor. These filmed television images, called *kinescopes*, were of relatively poor quality because of the difficulty in matching television images to film recording techniques, and only a few have survived to the present day, leaving a spotty record of television's pioneering years.

Television production was revolutionized in the mid-1950s by the introduction of *video tape*, which used magnetically coated tape to capture an analog of the television signal which would be played back at a later time. The quality of the video tape image was virtually identical to that of live television and it almost completely replaced it. Today, few television programs other than news and sporting events are broadcast live.

As noted in the last chapter, television programming has always been highly derivative of radio programming, with various genres of television programs (comedies, dramas, news broadcasts, game shows) scheduled in half hour and one hour blocks from the early morning to the late evening. Despite occasional programming innovations such as made-for-TV movies and mini-series, this remains true to the present day.

Early television channels all had frequencies in the so-called VHF (very high frequency) range, from 30 to 300 MHz (MHz stands for megahertz, or millions of cycles per second). On a television dial, these are stations with channel numbers between 2 and 13. (Channel 1 was dropped early on because its allocated frequencies interfered with certain non-television services.) In the mid-1950s, the FCC began allocating frequencies in the UHF (ultra-high frequency) range, from 300 to 3,000 MHz. Because higher frequency electromagnetic waves tend not to travel as far as lower frequency waves, these stations often had smaller audiences than

VHF stations. To reach larger audiences, many UHF stations utilized very powerful transmitters. However, this was costly. With the growth of cable television, many UHF stations now rely on cable to carry their signals to homes.

In the 1970s, broadcast television found itself with competition from an unexpected source. This new form of televised communication had its roots in an early 1950s phenomenon called *community antenna television* or *CATV* for short. In areas where television reception was poor, small businesses would erect large television antennas to draw in pictures from distant stations. Residents of the area would then hook into this antenna for a small fee, substantially improving television reception and increasing the number of channels that they could receive.

In time, community antenna television became known as *cable television,* but the initials CATV are still used. As the decades passed, CATV providers began adding their own programming in addition to the channels received over the antenna. Initially, this consisted primarily of channels featuring time and weather information, along with bulletin board channels featuring a continuous stream of paid and unpaid advertisements. In 1972, however, a nationwide service called Home Box Office (HBO) debuted, offering original programming to cable system owners—at a fee, of course. This initiated a new era of *cable-specific programming,* with dozens of cable television networks and local channels coming into existence.

Cable programming is, in general, less expensive to produce than network programming. (An exception to this is the so-called premium channels, such as HBO, Showtime, Home Team Sports, and so forth, which charge cable viewers an extra fee for high-quality entertainment such as recent movies, major sporting events, nightclub comedy, etc.) Because it is less expensive to produce, cable programming tends to be aimed at *niche markets*—narrower, more specific groups of viewers than those targeted by broadcast networks. Thus, we have such cable offerings as a children's network (Nickelodeon), a woman's network (Lifetime), a black-oriented network (Black Entertainment Television), a Hispanic network (Univision), all-music networks (MTV, VH1), an all-sports network (ESPN), business-oriented networks (Financial News Network, Consumer News and Business Channel), a religious network (The Interfaith Channel), and so forth.

Many observers have credited cable television with slowly eroding the viewership of the broadcast networks, though other media—prerecorded video tapes, for instance—have probably contributed. Nonetheless, the broadcast networks are still turning a healthy profit and will probably be with us for decades to come.

HDTV

The television systems in use today are essentially the same as those demonstrated more than half a century ago at the 1939 New York World's Fair. While other forms of electronic technology—the digital computer, for instance—have leaped ahead in sophistication during this period, television technology has stood nearly still since the introduction of color broadcasting in 1954. Incremental improvements such as self-adjusting pictures and remote-control tuners, along with such add-on devices as the home video recorder, have kept television competitive with other forms of electronic entertainment, but the quality of the television picture is far below that which electronic engineers are currently capable of producing.

The reason for the stagnation of television technology, of course, is the need to keep television broadcasting compatible with the huge number of televisions currently in the hands of consumers, not to mention the huge cost of converting television stations to a better system. But the pressure is gradually building on the television industry to change over to a system that would produce television pictures comparable in detail to high quality movie images, with wide screens similar to those used to view Cinemascope films. Such high-resolution, wide-screen television systems have been given the generic name of *high-definition television* or *HDTV* for short.

Much of the pressure comes from Japan, where an HDTV system is already in regular use. Members of the U.S. Congress have argued that, in order to remain technologically competitive with Japan, the United States must move toward HDTV broadcasting in the near future. Unfortunately, few of those concerned are able to agree on the nature of the HDTV system that U.S. broadcasters should adopt.

One solution might be to adopt the Japanese system, which is already in place. However, it would not be compatible with existing television systems, so that viewers would have to buy new televisions in order to watch high definition broadcasts. (By contrast, color television broadcasts are perfectly compatible with black-and-white televisions; only the color is lost on a black-and-white set.) Furthermore, some experts claim that the Japanese system is insufficiently high in quality to make the switch worthwhile.

More likely, the HDTV system adopted in the United States will be compatible with existing televisions, with additional scanning lines and extra portions of the picture broadcast on different frequencies from the regular picture. These scanning lines and picture portions would then be mixed together by the HDTV receiver to form a picture with (at least) twice as many raster lines as a conventional television and a wider image. Viewers who have seen experimental HDTV systems claim that the result is a surprisingly realistic picture.

Unfortunately, HDTV channels would take up a tremendous amount of electromagnetic bandwidth, limiting the number of HDTV broadcasting channels that would be available. These limitations would not apply to cable systems, however, or to programs distributed on pre-recorded video tapes, so HDTV may well be available through these media before broadcast HDTV becomes a reality.

PART TWO
DIGITAL
TELECOMMUNICATIONS

6
DIGITAL
INFORMATION

All of the systems that we have talked about so far for transmitting sound and pictures—telephone, radio and television—are analog systems. All involve creating an electric current that is an analog of the information being transmitted—that is, the current rises when some aspect of that information, such as sound frequency or picture brightness, rises and falls when that aspect falls. Electromagnetic communications systems such as radio and television use this electric current to create an electromagnetic wave that is also an analog for the information being transmitted.

The problem with analog information transmission is that even small errors in creating and reproducing the analog signal (be that signal electric or electromagnetic in nature) lead to small errors in the final result of the communication—and such errors can add up. A slight mishap in the transmission of an electric current representing a sound results in a slight loss of quality in the sound

95

itself, as reproduced at the other end of the transmission.

Every time an analog signal changes form—when going from sound wave to electric current and back again, or when being amplified, or when being translated from electric current to electromagnetic wave, etc.—there is opportunity for error. And, indeed, the errors always occur. It is impossible to precisely duplicate the original signal. And, so, the sound or picture that reaches the listener or viewer is never perfect—and is usually nowhere near so. Look at a television picture and you'll see that it is full of tiny flashes and shadows that don't belong. Music on the radio, especially on AM but even on FM, never sounds as good as a real orchestra. Something is always lost in the translation.

It is a truism in engineering that the simpler something is, the less likely it is to fail, if only because there are fewer things that can go wrong. An analog signal is an extremely complicated thing and something invariably goes wrong with it (which is why, for instance, videotaped movies inevitably degrade in quality when you make copies of them). If it were possible to broadcast sounds and pictures using a simpler kind of signal, we might actually get better results.

The simplest kind of signal that we've studied so far in this book was that used by the original Morse telegraph. It consisted of two types of electric pulses: dots and dashes. In theory, it would be possible to construct a telegraph that would never make mistakes at all, because of the simplicity of the system, while a mistake-proof system using analog signals is unimaginable.

Yet all that Morse's telegraph was good for was sending Morse code messages. It couldn't send sound or pictures. In fact, you might be tempted to say that it would be impossible to use a telegraph-like system to send anything as complex as a sound wave or a moving image.

But you would be wrong.

INFORMATION PROCESSING DEVICES

We stated earlier that the major problem with the telegraph, from the point of view of the general public, was that you needed to know Morse code in order to use it. And if you were to use it with any efficiency, you needed to be a trained and experienced operator, who practically talked in Morse code.

But what if there were a machine that could create and translate coded messages so quickly and efficiently that the trained operator were unnecessary? Furthermore, what if this machine were so fast in operation and so cleverly designed that it could use a simple code to transmit not only the letters of the alphabet, but sounds and pictures as well? And what if this machine could translate these codes back into sounds and pictures so rapidly and transparently that we would think we were listening to the radio or watching television?

In fact, there is such a machine. It's called the *digital computer.*

When the first modern computers were built in the 1940s and 1950s, the general public saw them primarily as glorified calculators, useful mainly for adding up columns of numbers and calculating the trajectories of guided missiles. (This was years before such obviously non-numeric computer applications as word processing and video games.) But computers aren't just number crunchers.

A mainframe computer system

What is a computer, then? It's a generic information processing device. That is, you can put any kind of information—in theory, at least—into a computer and get any kind of information back out. The type of information that you get back out depends on the type of information that you put in, but it is not the same information. It is changed in some way by having passed through the computer. The way in which it changes depends on how the computer has been *programmed*, that is, how it has been previously instructed to deal with the information. Given the right kinds of devices for getting information into and out of the computer, and given the right program (set of instructions), a computer can convert any kind of information into any other kind of information.

98

To see the significance of this, let's examine some other types of information processing devices. A piano, for instance, can be looked at as an information processing device that takes information from fingers pressing on keys and converts it into rhythmic patterns of waves in air, or *music*. Similarly, a typewriter converts the movement of fingers on keys into patterns of words on paper. A thermostat converts changes in air temperature into changes in the behavior of a heat pump. A phonograph converts patterns of grooves on the surface of a vinyl LP into patterns of sound in the air, while a CD player converts tiny pits on a silvered surface into sound and a cassette player converts patterns of magnetic particles in liquid emulsion into sound.

All telecommunications devices are information processing devices. A television camera converts patterns of light into electricity, while a television set converts the patterns in electricity back into patterns in light. A radio converts electromagnetic patterns into sound, and so forth.

In theory, a computer can play the role of any other information processing device. All it needs is the proper *input device* (for getting information into the computer), the proper *output device* (for getting the processed information back out of the computer), and the proper program (to tell it what to do with the information while it is passing through).

A computer equipped with a typist's keyboard, a printer, and word processing software can play the role of a typewriter, for instance. A computer equipped with a musical keyboard, a speaker, and music composition software can play the role of a piano. And a computer equipped with devices to detect electric currents or electromagnetic radiation, a video display to produce pictures and a speaker for sound, could play the role of a telephone, a radio, or a television.

The question that might come to mind at this point is, Why? What would be the advantage of having a computer play the role of a communications device when we already have perfectly good telephones, radios and television doing the job on their own?

There are several answers to that question. One is that by changing a computer's program (or *software*) it is possible to make it do things that telephones, radios, and televisions have never done before—without making any changes at all to the computer's hardware. Another reason is that computers deal with information in a much simpler form than analog information processing devices such as telephones, radios, and televisions do, a form that is much closer to the sort of information that telegraph systems deal with. And because this *digital* form of information is so much simpler than analog forms, it is less subject to errors and general degradation. In fact, it is possible to transmit digital information over long distances, amplifying it and converting it into various forms, without any loss of quality at all. This simply isn't possible with analog information.

Note that we are not suggesting that personal computers of the sort you probably have at your home or in your school will actually be converted into telephones, televisions and radios (though in some cases this may be precisely what happens, as we will see in Chapter Eight). Rather, we mean that more and more telephones, televisions and radios will be built with computers already inside them, in forms that you might not recognize as computers. And that the information these devices will be processing will be in digital form—that is, will be computer data—rather than analog.

A personal computer system,
complete with modem for data transmission
over telephone lines

BINARY DATA

In Chapter Two, we saw that the simplest information that can be carried by an electric current is whether or not the current is flowing, that is, whether the current is on or off. And that simple information can be controlled by a simple device: a switch.

Analog information is more complicated, depending not only on whether the current is on or off, but how strong the current is. Analog information is *too* complicated, so let's go back to the simpler information provided by an on-off switch.

An on-off switch would not seem to provide very much information, but that's not so. Virtually any type of information at all can be conveyed by an on-off switch, if we use it enough times. And if we know how to interpret the position of the switch.

For instance, we could say that a switch in the on position represents the word *yes* and a switch in the off position represents the word *no*. In that way, an on-off switch (attached, perhaps, to a light bulb) could be used to answer any yes-or-no question that you choose to ask. There is a game, for instance, called Twenty Questions, in which a player must guess what thing another player is thinking about by asking twenty yes-or-no questions. Such a game could be played using an on-off switch to answer the questions. In a sense, the on-off switch would tell the guessing player which object out of millions of objects in the world the other player was thinking of—a lot of information for a simple switch to convey.

An on-off switch can also represent numbers. We can say, for instance, that a switch in the off position represents the number zero and a switch in the on position represents the number one. But what if we wanted to represent numbers larger than one? Well, we could play a guessing game along the lines of Twenty Questions, with one player asking yes-or-no questions like, "Is the number larger than two?" Or "Is the number smaller than or equal to four?" In that way, it would take an average of two guesses (and two switches) to determine a number in the range zero to three and three guesses to determine a number in the range zero to seven.

There is, however, an easier (if closely related) way to represent numbers with an on-off switch. It's called the *binary numbering system*. You may have encountered it already, in studying computers or math.

To understand binary, however, we'll need to think of our on-off switch as representing the digits 0 and 1. If it makes you feel more comfortable, you can think of the phrase "switch in the off position" whenever we refer to 0 and "switch in the on position" whenever we refer to the digit 1. However, you'll probably find it easier to think in terms of digits rather than switches.

In the decimal numbering system that we normally use for counting, there are ten digits: 0 through 9. All decimal numbers are made up out of some combination of these digits. In a decimal number such as 5,823, the digit farthest to the right is equal to its normal value, while the digit to the left of it is worth ten times its normal value, the digit to the left of that is worth one hundred times its normal value, and the digit to the left of that is worth one thousand times its normal value. In other words, each digit position is worth ten times the value of the digit position to its right, multiplied by the digit in that position. That's why the decimal numbering system is also called *base ten*.

The binary numbering system, also known as *base two*, works the same way, except that each digit position is worth two times the value of the digit position to its right, multiplied by the digit in that position. (Remember that only the digits 0 and 1 are allowed.) Thus, in the binary number 11101101, the right-most digit position would be equal to 1 times 1 or 1, the next position would be equal to 0 times 2 or 0, the third position to 1 times 4 or 4, the fourth position to 1 times 8 or 8, the fifth position to 0 times 16 or 0, the sixth position to 1 times 32 or 32, the seventh position to 1 times 64 or 64, and the eighth position to 1 times 128 or 128. We then add these values together to get the decimal value of 1101101:

$$1 + 0 + 4 + 8 + 0 + 32 + 64 = 229$$

Thus, we could transmit the number 229 with only 8 flicks of an on-off switch—assuming the person at the other end of the electric circuit knew that we were using the binary numbering system.

Computers use the binary numbering system almost exclusively—on the inside, at least. (When a computer prints out a number on paper or on a video display it usually prints it in decimal, which is easier for human beings to understand.) Inside the computer are literally millions of tiny switches, not the mechanical kind used to turn light bulbs on and off but electronic switches represented by electric currents in miniscule circuits of conducting materials. So small are these switches that they can barely be seen even with the aid of a microscope.

Most computers are designed to handle binary numbers eight binary digits (or *bits*, for short) at a time. An eight-bit binary number is called a *byte*. (In addition, a four-bit binary number is called a *nybble*, a sixteen-bit binary number is called a *word*, a thirty-two-bit binary number is called a *long word* or *double word* and a sixty-four-bit binary number is called a *quad word*.) Because the largest possible eight bit number, 11111111, is equivalent to the decimal number 255, this gives us a range of 256 possible numbers to work with. (The 256th number is 0 itself.)

If we need a wider range of numbers to work with, we can slap two bytes together to form a sixteen-bit word. The largest possible sixteen-bit word is 1111111111111111, which is equivalent to the decimal number 65,535. This gives us a range of 65,536 words to work with. If we need an even larger range, we can keep slapping bytes together until we have enough.

Once we've gotten information into the form of binary numbers, we can process it with any digital computer. (The term "digital" simply refers to the use of binary digits to represent information. All modern computers are digital.) Getting information into binary form is the job of computer input devices. A keyboard, for instance, translates the movement of fingers on keys into binary numbers inside the computer. The role of output devices, in turn, is to translate those binary numbers back into a form recognizable to humans.

Although binary numbers are treated as on-off switches while inside a computer, this is not the only way in which binary numbers can be represented. Virtually anything that can take two possible positions or have two different values can represent binary numbers. For instance, we often need to store computer data outside the computer on magnetic disks or tape. The orientation of the magnetic particles on the surface of the disk or tape is what represents the binary numbers here. Groups of particles with one orientation represent ones, while groups of particles with a distinctly different orientation represent zeroes. Similarly, if we need to send binary data down an electric wire, we can represent zeroes as a low-voltage electric current and ones as a high-voltage electric current (or vice versa). And if we want to send binary data over the airwaves, we can use high-amplitude waves to represent ones and low-amplitude waves to represent zeroes.

When information is represented in analog form, it is the precise value of the analog representation—the strength of the current, the orientation of the magnetic particle, the amplitude of the electromagnetic wave—that represents the state of the information. Tiny changes in that value represent tiny changes in the information. When information is represented in binary form, on the other hand, only two values matter: high voltage or low voltage, one orientation or the other orientation, high amplitude or low amplitude, 0 or 1. Tiny changes are irrelevant. They don't affect the information. Thus, we don't have to worry about tiny imperfections in transmission of the information.

What we do have to worry about, though, is how the information is represented. So far, we have only seen how to represent numbers in binary. How do we represent sound and pictures and other types of information we might wish to transmit?

The answer is simple. We represent them as numbers, too—as we'll see in the next chapter.

7
FUN WITH BINARY DIGITS

There are nearly an infinite number of ways to represent information digitally. Several of these methods are now in common use. In this chapter, we'll look at several of those methods, to give you a feel for how information can be transmitted as binary numbers. Bear in mind, however, that there are far more methods of binary information representation than we have space to list here, and new methods are being invented all the time. Perhaps you'll invent a method of your own someday.

THE AMERICAN STANDARD CODE FOR INFORMATION INTERCHANGE (ASCII)

The American Standard Code for Information Interchange (ASCII, pronounced ASK KEY) was developed by a committee in the 1950s as a means of transmitting written text between computers and between computers and other devices, such as printers and video displays. It is a descendant of an earlier, five-bit binary code called the *Baudot code* used for transmitting data between teleprinters. The ASCII code represents the letters of the alphabet (both uppercase and lowercase), standard punctuation marks and several non-printing "characters" such as carriage returns and tabs as seven-bit binary numbers (giving ASCII a range of 0 to 127). The chart in Figure 11 shows the complete ASCII code. Most of the characters represented by the numbers in the range 0 to 32 are esoteric computer codes.

ASCII is such a common method of representing text that computer programs such as word processors almost invariably use some variation on ASCII to store text inside the computer and to transmit text to devices such as printers. In telecommunications, ASCII is commonly used for transmitting information between home computers and information services of the type that we'll be describing in the next chapter.

Although the ASCII code uses seven-bit binary numbers, ASCII information is usually stored and transmitted as eight-bit binary numbers. In part, this is simply because computers are more comfortable dealing with information in this form, but it also allows the eighth bit to be used to trap information errors, as we will see later in this chapter.

BITMAPS

Representing pictures as numbers is a little more complicated than representing text. The simplest, and probably most common, method of representing pictures in binary is the *bitmap*.

Computer pictures—or any other electronically represented picture, for that matter—are made up

The following is	33 – !	70 – F	107 – k
a complete listing	34 – "	71 – G	108 – l
of ASCII codes	35 – #	72 – H	109 – m
	36 – $	73 – I	110 – n
0 – Null	37 – %	74 – J	111 – o
1 – Start Heading	38 – &	75 – K	112 – p
2 – Start Text	39 – '	76 – L	113 – q
3 – End Text	40 – (	77 – M	114 – r
4 – End Transmit	41 –)	78 – N	115 – s
5 – Enquiry	42 – *	79 – O	116 – t
6 – Acknowledge	43 – +	80 – P	117 – u
7 – Bell (signal)	44 – ,	81 – Q	118 – v
8 – Backspace	45 – -	82 – R	119 – w
9 – Horiz. Table	46 – .	83 – S	120 – x
10 – Line Feed	47 – /	84 – T	121 – y
11 – Vertical Tab	48 – 0	85 – U	122 – z
12 – Form Feed	49 – 1	86 – V	123 – {
13 – Carriage Ret.	50 – 2	87 – W	124 –	
14 – Shift Out	51 – 3	88 – X	125 – }
15 – Shift In	52 – 4	89 – Y	126 – ~
16 – Data Link Esc.	53 – 5	90 – Z	127 – Delete
17 – Dev. Control 1	54 – 6	91 – [	
18 – Dev. Control 2	55 – 7	92 – \	
19 – Dev. Control 3	56 – 8	93 –]	
20 – Dev. Control 4	57 – 9	94 – ^	
21 – Neg. Ackhowl.	58 – :	95 – —	
22 – Synch. Idle	59 – ;	96 – (space)	
23 – End Tran Block	60 – <	97 – a	
24 – Cancel	61 – =	98 – b	
25 – End of Medium	62 – >	99 – c	
26 – Substitute	63 – ?	100 – d	
27 – Escape	64 – @	101 – e	
28 – File Separate	65 – A	102 – f	
29 – Group Separ.	66 – B	103 – g	
30 – Record Separ.	67 – C	104 – h	
31 – Unit Separate	68 – D	105 – i	
32 – Space	69 – E	106 – j	

Figure 11. The ASCII code

of *pixels* (short for pictorial elements; in television the term *pel* is sometimes used instead). The pixel is the smallest unit of detail in the picture; nothing smaller can be displayed. In a black-and-white picture, a pixel must be either black or white. In a color picture, it can be any color that the electronic device displaying the picture is capable of generating.

A bitmap is a sequence of binary numbers where every binary digit, or group of binary digits, corresponds to one of the pixels in a picture. In a black-and-white bitmap, a bit with a value of 1 typically indicates that the corresponding pixel is black and a bit with a value of 0 indicates that the corresponding pixel is white. In a color bitmap, several bits correspond with each pixel. In a four-color bitmap, for instance, two bits correspond to each pixel, with each of the four possible two-bit binary numbers representing one of the four colors. The more bits per pixel, the wider the range of colors that can be represented. Eight bits per pixel, for instance, would allow a 256-color bitmap.

Here is a simple black-and-white bitmap of a happy face:

```
000000000000000000000000
000000000001111000000000
000000011100001110000000
000000100000000001000000
000001000100001000100000
000001000100001000100000
000001000000000000100000
000001001000000100100000
000000100011110001000000
000000011100001110000000
000000000001111000000000
000000000000000000000000
```

Although this bitmap is too small to be of any practical use, it could be part of a larger bitmap. A typical bitmap for the image on higher resolution video displays of today's microcomputers might contain 100,000 or so bytes. A bitmap for a television picture would contain at least half a million bytes.

NORTH AMERICAN PRESENTATION LEVEL PROTOCOL SYNTAX (NAPLPS)

The main problem with bitmaps as a method of storing pictures is that they tend to be very large. Transmitting the bitmap for just one picture takes quite a long time and storing a picture in a computer takes a great deal of memory. A simpler method of representing a picture in binary is to represent so-called *graphics primitives*—lines, circles, patterns, etc.—as numbers, the way that the ASCII code represents letters of the alphabet as numbers.

The *North American Presentation Level Protocol Syntax* (*NAPLPS*, pronounced NAP-LIPS) is an extension of the ASCII code devised by a committee in the early 1980s. It is a set of several codes, including ASCII, for representing information visually. More than one of these codes, for instance, consists of eight-bit binary numbers that represent drawing operations, such as "draw a circle with a radius of n," where n is the number following the number representing the instruction, or "fill an area measuring x by y with pattern z," where x, y, and z are the numbers following the instruction, or "begin drawing in color n," and so forth. In other codes, each number represents a small mosaic "tile" that can be used to build a larger picture. Certain numbers in each code are reserved for switching between codes.

A properly designed sequence of NAPLPS code numbers can be used for drawing pictures and text on a computer screen. Because NAPLPS does not require that every pixel in an image be transmitted as a bit or set of bits, it requires fewer bytes of data to create a picture. This greatly speeds up the amount of time needed to transmit a NAPLPS picture and reduces the amount of computer memory (internal circuits) needed to store it.

There are other coding systems, similar to NAPLPS, that can be used for storing and transmitting pictures. One, called Display Postscript, is based on the Postscript computer language, more commonly used for transmitting pictures to a computer printer.

DIGITAL SOUND

How can we represent sound in binary? Remember from Chapter Three that a sound wave can be represented as a rising and falling line, as in Figure 12. If we then imagine a horizontal line running just below the lowest trough of the sound wave, which we can call the *baseline*, we can look at each point on the sound wave as having a certain height above the baseline, which we can measure using some arbitrary unit.

Figure 13 shows a sound wave with lines measuring the height of the sound wave in units at even intervals. We can then describe the sound wave as a series of numbers, which can later be used to reproduce the sound wave, rather like a connect-the-dots puzzle. This process, which can be performed electronically by connecting a microphone or other analog sound device to an *analog-to-digital converter* (*ADC* for short), is called *digital sampling*. Each individual measurement of the sound wave is called a *sample;* if we take our samples

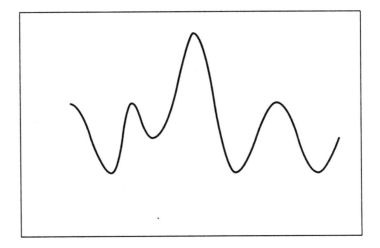

Figure 12. Sound wave represented as a rising and falling line

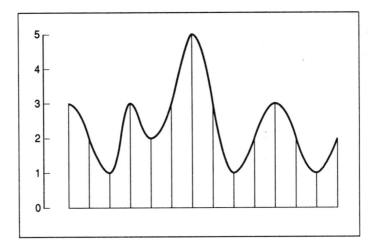

Figure 13. We can describe sound as a series of numbers by measuring the heights of the waves at regular intervals. This is known as digital sampling.

often enough—on the order of 40,000 times a second, say—we can then use an electronic device to reconstruct the sound wave so nearly perfectly that our ears can't tell the difference between the original sound wave and the reconstruction.

This is essentially the method used to create *compact discs (CDs)*, for instance. Although compact discs are beyond the scope of this book, they use a purely digital representation of a sound wave to store and reproduce that wave—and the results are often breathtaking. It is also possible to store digitally recorded sound as a series of binary numbers in a computer or on a magnetic computer disk—and to transmit those sounds using any method suitable for transmitting computer data. (Note that computer *disk* is spelled differently from a compact *disc*.)

An array of digital storage optical disks

114

These are only four possible ways of representing information digitally; as we said, there are many other methods, with no doubt more to come. This should give you the flavor of binary information representation.

Now let's turn to two more of the reasons why we would want to use digital information in the first place: digital error detection and digital error correction.

ERROR DETECTION AND ERROR CORRECTION

We saw earlier that, because of its simplicity, digital data can be transmitted very accurately. Small changes in the representation of digital data don't affect the accuracy of the data at all. Nonetheless, larger errors can occur—a 1 can be mistaken for a 0 or vice versa. One of the great advantages of digital information is that such errors can still be caught—and even corrected.

The simplest method of digital error detection is *parity checking*. Suppose we are transmitting a stream of ASCII codes from one computer to another. The ASCII code uses seven-bit binary numbers, but we are quite probably using eight-bit binary numbers in our transmission. Thus, we are free to use the eighth bit as a *parity bit*. If we are using the system called *even parity*, the computer transmitting the data will count the number of 1 bits in each byte. If there are an even number of 1 bits, it will set the 8th bit (which is not used in the code) to a 0. If there are an odd number of 1 bits, it will set the eighth bit to a 1, making the number even. This guarantees that all of the eight-bit numbers leaving the transmitting computer will have an even number of 1 bits in them. (If *odd par-*

ity is being used, the computer will check for odd numbers of 1 bits rather than even.)

The receiving computer checks each incoming code number to see if it has an even number of 1 bits. If it does, the receiving computer simply ignores the eighth bit (because it isn't part of the actual data). If it does not, the receiving computer knows that an error must have occurred in transmission, changing a 1 to a 0 or vice versa, and sends a message to the transmitting computer asking it to send the code again.

Parity checking is not a very accurate method of error detection. If two bits are changed in a single code, for instance, the parity will still be even and the error will go undetected. For serious data transmissions, more accurate methods of error detection are required.

When using a *checksum*, data is sent from the transmitting computer to the receiving computer in standard size *blocks*, usually between 128 and 1024 bytes long. While it is sending a block of data, the transmitting computer adds up all the bytes and saves the sum. (Actually, it usually only saves the last 8 or 16 bits in the sum.) At the end of the block, it transmits this sum to the receiving computer. Meanwhile, the receiving computer has been keeping its own total of the bytes in the block. When it gets the sum from the other computer, it compares it with its own sum. If they match, then the receiving computer knows that the data in the block are correct. If they don't match, then there has been an error and the receiving computer sends a message to the sending computer, asking it to transmit the block again.

Checksums are not 100 percent reliable, but they catch most errors. There is a variation on the checksum called the *cyclical redundancy check (CRC)* that performs more complex operations on the bytes in the block than just addition. The CRC is somewhat more accurate than the checksum.

Error detection methods can catch most errors in digital transmission, but they are only appropriate in situations where it is possible to ask the transmitter to send the data again. This isn't always the case. It is not likely, for instance, that a television set will be in a position to ask a television station to send a picture twice. What is needed in this case is a method of *error correction*, that is, a method by which the receiving computer can not only detect errors in the transmission but correct them without asking for a retransmission.

At first encounter, this might seem like an impossible deal, but it isn't really. The trick is to add *redundancy*, sending more information than is actually needed. If some of the information is lost, the missing part can be reconstructed from the part that isn't lost. Only if more than a certain percentage of the data is lost will the errors be uncorrectable. Thus, it's necessary to study the amount of noise (i.e., potential errors) on a transmission channel and add sufficient redundancy to the data to make it correctable despite the errors.

Let's consider a really noisy data channel: the empty space between earth and the planets Jupiter, Saturn, Uranus, and Neptune. As the spacecraft *Voyager 2* sailed into the outer reaches of the solar system, it continued sending back bit-mapped pictures of the outer planets. The stream of bytes that constituted this color bitmap was subject to interference from extraneous sources both inside and outside the earth's atmosphere. And as the spacecraft got farther away, the signal grew weaker and weaker, increasing the probability of transmission errors.

Decimal	Binary	Reed–Muller Code
000	00000	00000000000000000000000000000000
001	00001	01010101010101010101010101010101
002	00010	00110011001100110011001100110011
003	00011	01100110011001100110011001100110
004	00100	00001111000011110000111100001111
005	00101	01011010010110100101101001011010
006	00110	00111100001111000011110000111100
007	00111	01101001011010010110100101101001
008	01000	00000000111111110000000011111111
009	01001	01010101101010100101010110101010
010	01010	00110011110011000011001111001100
011	01011	01100110100110010110011010011001
012	01100	00001111111100000000111111110000
013	01101	01011010101001010101101010100101
014	01110	00111100110000110011110011000011
015	01111	01101001100101100110100110010110
016	10000	00000000000000001111111111111111
017	10001	01010101010101011010101010101010
018	10010	00110011001100111100110011001100
019	10011	01100110011001101001100110011001
020	10100	00001111000011111111000011110000
021	10101	01011010010110101010010110100101
022	10110	00111100001111001100001111000011
023	10111	01101001011010011001011010010110
024	11000	00000000111111111111111100000000
025	11001	01010101101010101010101001010101
026	11010	00110011110011001100110000110011
027	11011	01100110100110011001100101100110
028	11100	00001111111100001111000000001111
029	11101	01011010101001011010010101011010
030	11110	00111100110000111100001100111100
031	11111	01101001100101101001011001101001

Figure 14. Reed-Muller codes for
five-bit binary numbers

Understanding that they were broadcasting
through an unusually noisy channel, NASA engineers programmed Voyager to transmit each five-
bit binary number in the bitmap back to earth as
a thirty-two-bit *Reed-Muller code*. There are thirty-
two of these thirty-two-bit codes, shown in Figure
14, each of which corresponds to one possible five-

bit number. These codes are deliberately chosen so that no two codes differ from one another in less than eight digit positions. (This is called the *Hamming distance* between the codes.) Thus, if as many as seven bits in a thirty-two-bit number are altered in transmission, the original number can still be reconstructed by choosing the code number that has the most digits in common with the number received. Only if eight or more digits are wrong will the error be uncorrectable.

Error correcting systems like this can be used to correct errors in any kind of digital data transmission or data storage. Compact discs, for instance, use error correction codes that will catch all but one error in every two compact discs. CD-ROMS, which are compact discs used to store computer data, use an even more stringent error correction code that will catch all but one error in every 2,000 discs. The price of these error correction codes is that the redundant information required by the codes takes up a lot of storage space and slows down transmissions considerably. But if accuracy of data transmission is required, this price may be worth paying.

In this chapter we've looked at some of the theoretical reasons for using digital information transmission. In the next chapter, we'll look at some of the situations where digital communications are actually used—and some of the places where they will be used in the future.

8
DIGITAL COMMUNICATIONS: NOW AND THEN

In theory, we could convert all existing communications systems to digital. We would have digital television, digital radio, digital telephones. We would enjoy pictures and sound clearer than any we had ever seen and heard on television and radio before. Alas, converting to digital will be a long and expensive process. The only one of these systems that is likely to take extensive advantage of digital information transmission in the near future is the telephone system, as we will see later in this chapter.

But digital methods will spawn new media, a process that has already begun. One of the advantages of these new telecommunications media is that they have the potential to be *interactive*. Because the device with which we are receiving the communication and the device that is sending the communication are both computers, there is the possibility that we can use our computer to talk back to their computer. In the case of the telephone, this hardly seems surprising; we are accustomed to talking back to the telephone. But someday you may also be able to talk back to your television and radio as well.

COMPUTER TELECOMMUNICATIONS

One new medium that is already available to anyone with a personal computer is *computer telecommunications*. In effect, all you need to do is plug your computer into your telephone, run a *communications program*, and start talking to computers far away.

Of course, plugging your computer into your telephone is easier said than done. Telephone lines aren't designed for carrying digital data. So you'll also need a device called a *modem* that will allow you to transmit digital data over ordinary phone lines.

Modem is short for *modulator-demodulator*, because the modem modulates the sound waves going out over the telephone and demodulates the sound waves coming back. Your computer transmits digital electrical signals (high-voltage signal equaling one and low-voltage signal equaling zero) to the modem over a *serial cable*. The modem converts these signals into tones, which travel over the telephone like any other sound. When using a slower modem, a high-pitched tone represents a one and a low-pitched tone represents zero. A modem at the other end of the line converts these tones back into binary electrical signals.

(Actually, four tones are usually used, with the modem at one end of the line using two tones to represent zero and one and the modem at the other end of the line using two different tones to represent zero and one. This allows the two computers

122

to talk simultaneously on the line without getting confused.)

The number of tones transmitted over the telephone per second is called the *baud rate*. The number of binary bits transmitted per second is called the *bits per second* or bps rate. Since, on a slower modem, the number of tones is the same as the number of bits per second, these numbers are the same. On faster modems, however, this is not the case.

The slowest modems run at a speed of 300 baud and 300 bps. This is considered quite slow. Unfortunately, standard telephone lines can't handle more than about 600 tones per second, or 600 baud, which isn't much faster. Thus, to transmit at higher bps rates, it is necessary to transmit more bits per baud.

When 300 baud modems convert binary digits into tones on a telephone they are using a form of frequency modulation: the frequency of the tone represents the 1s and 0s of the binary data. If we mix in a little phase modulation along with the frequency modulation, we can actually make each tone sufficiently different from other tones at the same frequency that each tone can represent up to four binary digits. That way, we can make a 300-baud modem transmit and receive 1,200 bits per second. And, in fact, this is the method used to design 1,200-bps modems (sometimes incorrrectly called 1,200-baud modems). Similarly, we can design 600 baud modems that transmit and receive 2,400 bps.

Higher speed modems require even more complicated methods of squeezing extra bits into each baud. Modems are available that can transmit and receive at speeds of 9,600 and even 14,400 bps; using special *data compression* techniques that squeeze more digital information into a limited number of bytes, speeds upwards of 20,000 bps can be achieved in a few cases. But as of this writing there is no one standard method for producing such high data rates, which means that computers using one brand of modem might not be able to communicate with computers using a different brand of modem. By the time you read this book, this situation may have changed and 9,600 bps modems may be common. But presently the standard modem speed is 2,400 bps.

INFORMATION SERVICES

Assuming that you have a computer with a modem attached to it, whom can you talk to? There are quite a few other computers out there eager to talk with yours. In fact, you might be surprised at how many there are.

There are more than several dozen commercial information services available to computer users willing to pay a subscription rate. Usually, this involves paying a fee for each minute spent on line, though at least one current service charges a fixed fee for unlimited *connect time*. To access these services, you hook up your modem, run a communications program and ask your computer to dial their telephone number. You can usually register to use the service on-line and pay for it with a credit card or some other billing arrangement. At the time of registration you are given a user number and a password, which you will be asked for each time you *log on* to the service.

Some of the best-known information services are Compuserve, GEnie (from General Electric), Delphi, Prodigy (from IBM and Sears), PC Link and Dow Jones. Typically, these services offer on-line

```
M 301

*  Nobles desired to absorb unowned  *
   planets.  Type "GALAXY" to play!
GEnie          REFERENCE         Page 301
          Reference Library

  1. Grolier's Encyclopedia
  2. CINEMAN Entertainment Information
  3. Hollywood Hotline TM Movie Reviews
  4. Rainbo Electronic Reviews
  5. PhotoSource International
  6. Medical RT
  7. Dr. Job
  8. Rensselaer Polytechnic RT
  9. NewsBytes News Service

Enter #, <P>revious, or <H>elp?
```

Subscribers to on-line information
services can select from a smorgasbord
of data bases. Such services can provide
everything from the latest stock
prices to movie reviews.

·

news and weather, access to *computer bulletin boards* (where you can exchange messages with other users), libraries of files (including computer programs) that can be sent directly to your computer over telephone lines, on-line shopping, and a great deal more. Most services are ASCII based, that is, information is transmitted between your computer and the service using ASCII codes. As you receive binary ASCII codes over the telephone lines, the communications program that you are using prints the corresponding text characters on the display of your computer. And, as you type on the computer's keyboard, the program transmits the codes for the characters that you type over the modem.

More recently, several services have begun using graphics-based code systems to display pictures on the video screen of users' computers. The Prodigy Service, for instance, uses the NAPLPS protocol described in the last chapter.

When transmitting files such as computer programs between computers (a process known as *downloading* or *uploading*, depending on the direction in which the files are being sent), special *file transfer protocols* are used. These special-purpose computer programs, which have names like Xmodem, Ymodem, Compuserve B, etc., break the data in the file into blocks and use checksums and CRCs to verify the accuracy of the data.

PRIVATE BBSES

The services described in the last section are commercial; that is, they charge you money for accessing their computers and taking advantage of the on-line services they offer. However, anyone with a computer, a modem, and a free telephone line can start his/her own on-line service. Such private services are called *bulletin board systems* or *BBSes* for short.

Usually, only one person at a time can call a private BBS, so expect plenty of busy signals if you want to take advantage of these bargain opportunities. Fortunately, most major cities have hundreds or even thousands of private BBSes within range of a local telephone call. If one is busy, just try another.

A typical BBS system will feature a message area where users can leave notes that others can read and reply to, an Electronic Mail system that lets you send private notes to specific users (and receive them as well), data libraries with files for download, on-line games, and a wealth of other features. Many of these features are also available on commercial services, but here they are free.

Most private BBSes are ASCII based, though some systems take advantage of special graphics features of specific personal computers and communications programs to add pictures and even animations to the features available on line.

ISDN

In the next century there will be a revolution in digital telecommunications, but it will not happen immediately. The digital revolution will be a slow revolution, occurring piece by piece, as various forms of telecommunications change from analog to digital transmission methods.

One part of this digital revolution is taking place right now, however, and it may totally alter the face of telecommunications in the early twenty-first century. (A few critics argue, on the other hand, that it may be the biggest flop of the late twentieth century.) It is called the *Integrated Systems Digital Network (ISDN)*. Conceived in the early 1970s by the *CCITT* (an acronym for a French name meaning *Consultative Committee for International Telephony and Telegraphy*), an international committee responsible for worldwide telecommunications standards, ISDN is a plan for the digitization of the telephone networks. But it is much more than a scheme for making digital telephone calls.

The American telephone network is already largely digital. In fact, the only analog part of the system are the lines, called the *local loop*, that connect the phone in your home with the local telephone switching station (which is itself almost entirely computerized). Unfortunately, it is these analog lines that require the use of a modem for the transmission of digital information; and it is these analog lines that introduce most of the extraneous noise into your telephone calls. If this part of the telephone system were digital, we could make telephone calls that (in theory) sounded as good as digitally recorded compact discs—and we could connect our modems to our computer via digital adapters that would communicate at speeds vastly higher than the 2,400 baud modems currently in common use.

This is the goal of ISDN. Already in place in several American cities (New York being a conspicuous exception), ISDN will use standard local telephone lines to provide digital service directly to homes and offices. It will be possible, using an ISDN adapter, to hook your computer directly to the telephone and transmit data at speeds of 64,000 bps—without a modem! (At this writing, however, the prices of these adapters are quite high, though this may change in the near future.)

Every ISDN subscriber will gain the use of three digital channels, a B channel (used by ISDN devices to exchange special control signals with the ISDN network itself) and two D channels (used for sending and receiving 64,000 bps transmissions, respectively). To make digital phone calls, it will also be necessary to own a digital telephone, or at least to use a digital adapter to make your current telephone compatible with ISDN.

Once these ISDN channels are in place, a number of special services will become available. The most widely advertised is Caller ID, which displays the number of the person calling you on an illuminated panel next to the phone. This allows you to screen your telephone calls and identify unwanted callers.

However, ISDN will also lead to higher quality telephone calls and more. Fax machines will work at least seven times faster than they do now, for instance. Video can be transmitted over the telephone, for a kind of computerized television. Picture-phones of the sort seen in movies like *2001: A Space Odyssey* will be an inexpensive reality. We will all be given permanent phone numbers, as we are now given Social Security numbers, and these numbers will follow us about wherever we go. When visiting distant places, we will simply punch our ISDN number into the nearest phone and receive our calls there.

Although the telephone company is currently advertising ISDN primarily as a means of getting Caller ID and similar services, many ISDN supporters see it as the beginning of a true revolution in digital communications. When a second generation of ISDN arrives in the next century, allowing communications at rates in the millions of BPS, the telephone network may become the center of a new form of communication that will combine the telephone with television, radio, video games, compact discs, even newspapers. All communication to the home may arrive over a single, television-like unit, with a computer built in. News broadcasts will be tailored to your interests by the computer and newspapers (if you prefer hard copy) will be printed out by laser printer. You'll be communicating with distant friends over the television, seeing them, talking to them, exchanging notes and recordings and computer programs with them.

This vision of centralized telecommunications may be far away, but it is also certainly coming. Once all information is in digital format—once it is all computer data—we will no longer need the artificial distinctions between various forms of telecommunications, such as radio, television and telephone. They will all be part of a giant telecommunications web that will come into our homes via phone lines and electromagnetic signals. They will follow us about on portable radios, TVs and telephones, where we will be contacted via our permanent phone numbers.

GLOSSARY

Amplitude—The height of a wave.

Amplitude modulation (AM)—Changing the amplitude of a wave so that it can carry a message.

Analog information transmission—The transmission of information via a medium that changes continuously in a manner "analogous" to the original source of the information.

Analog-to-digital converter (ADC)—A device for converting analog electrical signals to digital electrical signals.

Bandwidth—The range of values that can be used to encode information in a communications medium.

Baudot code—An early, five-bit binary code for transmitting data between teleprinters.

Baud rate—The number of tones produced per second by a modem and transmitted over a telephone; see *modem.*

Binary numbering system—A numbering system that uses only two digits, 0 and 1, to represent numbers.

131

Bit—The smallest unit of information; short for "binary digit," because a bit can be represented by either the digit 0 or 1.

Bitmap—A system for representing pictures as sequences of binary numbers.

Bits per second (bps)—The rate at which data is transmitted between computers and computer peripheral devices; sometimes incorrectly called "baud rate."

Canceling—The subtraction of the heights of a crest and a trough to form a lower crest or shallower trough.

Carrier wave—A wave that can be modulated to carry a message.

Cathode ray tube (CRT)—An electronic device that generates beams of electrons inside a vacuum-sealed container; used to create pictures in a television.

CATV—Short for either community antenna television or cable television.

Checksum—A method of verifying the accuracy of digital data.

Chrominance signal—The portion of the television signal that carries the three colors used to create the color image on the screen of a color TV.

Circuit—A circular stream of electricity.

Communications program—A computer program that allows data to be transmitted between two computers, assuming that the necessary hardware for the transmission is available.

Compact discs (CDs)—An information-recording medium for digital sound.

Complex wave—A wave formed by combining two or more sine waves.

Compression wave—A wave that moves back and forth in the same direction that it is traveling.

Computer bulletin boards—Telecommunications services available, often for free, to computer users that allow reading and writing messages to and from other users of the service.

Computer telecommunications—The transmission of data directly from one computer to another via telecommunications devices such as the telephone.

Conductor—See *electrical conductor*.

Crest—The highest point in a wave.

Cycles—The entire motion of a wave from one crest to the next.

Cyclical redundancy check (CRC)—A method for verifying the accuracy of digital data.

Data compression—Techniques used to reduce the size of digital data for transmission and storage.

Digital information transmission—The transmission of information as a series of discrete signals, or digits.

Digital sampling—A system for transmitting or recording sounds as a sequence of binary numbers representing the height of the sound wave at fixed points along its length.

Downloading—The transmission of a computer data file to your computer from a remote computer.

Electrical conductor—A substance through which electricity can flow.

Electromagnetic radiation—A wave that can travel through empty space; light is a form of electromagnetic radiation, as are radio waves, X rays, gamma rays, microwaves, etc.

Electron—An extremely small particle that is one of the fundamental building blocks for all matter.

Electron scanning gun—A device inside a television that fires beams of electrons at the phosphors inside the picture tube to create the picture.

Error correction—A set of methods for correcting errors in digital data.

133

Fourier transform—A mathematical technique devised by Jean-Baptiste Fourier for breaking a complex wave into its component sine waves.

Frequency—The number of wave crests that pass a given point in one second.

Frequency modulation (FM)—Selectively changing the frequency of a wave so that it can carry a message.

Graphics primitives—Simple instructions for creating a picture, which can be represented as binary numbers.

Hertz (Hz)—A measure of the frequency of a wave in "cycles per second."

High-definition television (HDTV)—Improved-quality television systems featuring larger and more detailed images.

Horizontal retrace—The repositioning of the electron scanning gun in a television picture tube from the right side of the screen to the left after a raster line is drawn and before the next line is drawn.

Input device—A device that moves information into a computer.

Interference—The combining of two waves to form a third wave reinforcing and canceling the characteristics of both.

Integrated Systems Digital Network (ISDN)—An international standard for the transmission of digital data over telephone lines.

Interlace—The system by which a television picture is transmitted in two "halves," each of which contains every other line of the picture.

Kinescopes—Archival recordings of early television programs filmed directly off television monitors.

Luminance signal—The portion of the television signal that contains the black-and-white image.

134

Modem—A device for translating the digital data produced by a computer into a series of tones that can be transmitted over an ordinary analog telephone; short for "modulator-demodulator."

Modulation—Changing a wave in such a way that it can carry a message.

Network—A system of two or more broadcasting outlets in different geographical locations that share the same programming.

Niche markets—Relatively small groups of viewers targeted by producers of inexpensive cable programming.

NTSC system—A standard system for encoding a television picture out of 525 interlaced scanning lines that are updated thirty times per second, used in the United States, Japan, and several other countries; short for National Television System Committee, the name of the organization that formulated the standard.

Output device—A device that moves information back out of a computer.

PAL system—A standard system for encoding a television picture out of 625 interlace scanning lines updated twenty-five times a second, used primarily in Europe; short for "phase alternating line."

Parity checking—A simple method for verifying the accuracy of digital data.

Phase—The position in space of a wave relative to other waves.

Phase modulation—Changing the phase of a wave so that it can carry a message.

Pickup tube—The area inside a TV camera where the light image that enters the camera through the lens is converted into an electric current.

Picture tube—See cathode ray tube.

Pixel—The smallest element of detail in a tele-

135

vision image; short for "pictorial element." Sometimes also called a *pel*.

Pulses—On/off electrical signals used to carry information.

Radiotelegraphy—The transmission of telegraphic messages through the air in the form of electromagnetic radiation.

Radiotelephony ("radio")—The transmission of sound information through the air in the form of electromagnetic radiation.

Raster lines—See *scanning lines.*

Reinforcing—The adding together of the heights of two wave crests (or troughs) to form a higher crest (or deeper trough).

Scanning lines—The glowing lines on the inside of a television screen that make up the television picture.

Sine wave—A kind of wave that rises and falls in a simple, repetitive pattern.

Sound waves—The waves that carry sound information through the air.

Standard broadcasting—Early name for AM radio broadcasting.

Static—Noise added to an information-carrying signal by extraneous waves.

Target plate—A metal plate inside a TV camera covered with a light-sensitive substance that converts the energy of the light striking it into electricity.

Transistor—A solid state device for controlling and amplifying an electrical current.

Transverse wave—A wave that rises and falls perpendicular to the direction in which it is traveling.

Trough—The lowest point in a wave.

Twisted-pair wires—A pair of wires twisted together in such a manner that one half of the pair can carry the current in one direction and the other can carry it back to complete the circuit.

Uploading—The transmission of a computer data file from your computer to a remote computer.

Vertical retrace—The repositioning of the electron scanning gun in a television picture tube from the bottom of the screen to the left after a complete picture is drawn.

Wavelength—The distance from one crest to the next in a wave (or from one trough to the next).

Wireless telegraphy—See *radiotelegraphy.*

FOR FURTHER READING

Barnouw, Erik. *A Tower in Babel: A History of Broadcasting in the United States to 1933*. New York: Oxford University Press, 1966.

Dewdney, A.K. *The Turing Omnibus: 61 Excursions in Computer Science*. Rockville, MD: Computer Science Press, 1989.

Dvorak, John C., and Nick Anis. *Dvorak's Guide to PC Telecommunications*. New York: McGraw-Hill, 1990.

Fox, Linda, ed., *Broadcasting and Communications*. New York: Arco, 1978.

Friend, George E., John L. Fike, H. Charles Baker, and John C. Bellamy. *Understanding Data Communications*. Indianapolis: Howard W. Sams, 1984.

Kittross, Sterling. *Stay Tuned: A Concise History of American Broadcasting*. Belmont, California: Wadsworth Publishing Company, 1978.

O'Reilly, J.J. *Telecommunication Principles (Second Edition)*. London: Van Nostrand Reinhold, 1989.

Smale, P.H. *Introduction to Telecommunications Systems.* Blue Ridge Summit, PA: TAB Books, 1986.

Whitehouse, George E. *Understanding the New Technologies of the Mass Media.* Englewood Cliffs, New Jersey: Prentice-Hall, 1986.

INDEX

Illustrations are indicated by italicized page numbers.

141

143